SECRET

CHARLOTTESVILLE

A Guide to the Weird, Wonderful, and Obscure

Marijean Oldham

Reedy Press
PO Box 5131
St. Louis, MO 63139
www.reedypress.com

Library of Congress Control Number: 2021935143
ISBN: 9781681063324

Design by Jill Halpin

Cover images courtesy: Fighters—Charlottesville Battle Gaming, Observatory—McCormick Observatory, Rock Maze—Wildrock, Mural—Marijean Oldham.
All other photos by the author unless otherwise noted.

Printed in the United States of America
21 22 23 24 25   5 4 3 2 1

For Seth, Aaron, Allison, Cyd, and Grey, who provide a constant
flow of love, ideas, and encouragement.

CONTENTS

ACKNOWLEDGMENTS

Writing a book during a global pandemic has its challenges! I'm grateful to the many people who were willing to meet at an appropriate social distance, to join me for Zoom sessions, to have long phone calls, or to respond to my many questions via email.

Thank you to Brendan Wolfe, the very first person I thought of when I began this project, for front-porch brainstorming with me in the earliest days and for continuing to check in throughout. Thanks to Sean McCord, who, among other things, was the gateway to Hoke Perkins, an excellent resource who took the time to tell me many fantastic stories.

Thanks to Aaron Jaggers, history enthusiast and educator, who drew from the experience of spending his formative years in Charlottesville to be an early source of inspiration for this book. He also happens to be my son.

Thanks to friends Amanda Doyle, Cary Oliva, Cindy Kirst, Dan Epstein, Jeff Uphoff, Ryan Looney, Sarah Keenan Harris, Pat and Jane Belisle, Karen Klick, Kate Duvall, Beth Duffy Cox, Aimee Carter, Travis Koshko, Heather Balmat, Carson Oldham, Courtney Polk, Susan Sherman, Amanda Hallstead Litchfield, and Jennifer Alluisi. Your support and interest in this project helped keep me going!

I'm grateful to community members who contributed thoughts, facts, photos, or ideas, among them: Peyton Williams, Erica Barga, Valerie Hill, Rob Craighurst, Erin O'Hare, Sam Bush, Sarah Crossland, Jeff Dubrow, Erin Hill, Roger Voisinet, Drew Thomassan, Travis Wilburn, Rochelle Garwood, Ricky Patterson, Joe Powers, Rebecca Flowers, Bill Curtis, Joe Compton, Chester Hull, Hunter Chorey, Jody Saunders, Andrew LaPrade, Lindsay Daniels, Kate Collier, Laura Byrnes, Alex Rebhorn, Melissa Garth Suttle, Cindy Hersman, Hannah Russell Davis, Beth Kennan, Kristin Clarens, Vijay Owens, Jamie Kurtz, Benjamin Randolph, Steve Houchens, Desiree Cafaro, and Edwin Roa.

Photographers tell such great stories, in pictures and in words. Thank you to Jack Looney, Tristan Williams, Stevan Michaels, and Rich Tarbell.

A special thanks to all the Redditors who like to post their opinions of Charlottesville.

My friends who were early readers and editors, Jennifer Brecht and Mary Sproles Martin, get heaps of praise for their input and editorial contributions. I couldn't have done it without you.

Extra appreciation for Seth Oldham, my adventure companion, getaway enabler, and enthusiastic supporter.

Without all of you, these secrets could never be told.

INTRODUCTION

Did the real Anastasia really walk among us? Did General Custer leave a pair of his boots here? Is this where Georgia O'Keeffe learned to paint? Is there a secret, Cold War military bunker nearby? Did Dr. Seuss build a house near the University of Virginia? Charlottesville is as rich in folklore as it is in history. My research for this book took me down rabbit holes familiar to some locals, but still a mystery to many.

I heard a lot of tall tales when I first came to Charlottesville in 2005, and since then have learned fascinating facts about the area's history.

This book is a guide for people who want to learn about and experience the hidden gems of Charlottesville, and who want to better understand what they see on our streets, in our neighborhoods, and around the countryside.

Secret Charlottesville covers more than what's within the city limits, extending its reach to Orange County, Crozet, North Garden, and Keswick. This book invites readers to explore mountains, trails, waterways, parks, city streets, and notable landmarks.

Interesting stories unfold around every corner. To dig into them, I talked to historians, journalists, people walking their dogs, friends, and friends of friends. I received input from community groups and read a lot of opinions and stories about what makes Charlottesville so special.

As I continue to explore and you do, too, I invite you to join me using #SecretCville on social media so we can share new finds and excellent secrets.

THE "IN" CROWD

What's more secret than secret societies?

Secret societies at the University of Virginia (UVa) are as old as the university itself. The oldest are the IMP Society, the Z Society, and the Seven Society, with the Sevens being the most secretive of all.

While some societies are formed to recognize accomplishments among their members, others, like The Sons and Daughters of Liberty, are known for pranks and shenanigans.

The Seven Society, like the IMPs and the Z Society, leaves its mark on buildings around campus. Look for the number 7 surrounded by the signs for alpha (A), omega (Ω), and infinity (∞), and several stars. A plaque with this symbol can be found outside Cabell Hall.

The Sevens are only revealed posthumously. A wreath of black magnolias in the shape of a seven appears at the gravesite of any member who has died. It's a mystery how these members keep their generosity a secret, as this society's main function is philanthropy to the university. Gifts always contain the number seven, the most generous of which was a donation of $777,777.77, establishing a grant allowing professors to teach courses they've always dreamed of teaching.

It's not just financial support that the Sevens provide. In August 2017, when hate-based organizations including the Ku Klux Klan and the Proud Boys congregated on the Grounds* of the university, a banner appeared. Its message: "Our mission therefore is to confront ignorance with knowledge, bigotry with

---

Need to get in touch with the Seven Society? It's said that if you place a letter in the crook of the arm of the Thomas Jefferson statue at the University's Rotunda, the society will receive your message.

Membership in the secret societies at UVa is a lifelong honor and commitment. Members are often not revealed until after they are deceased.

tolerance, and isolation with the outstretched hand of generosity. Racism can, will, and must be defeated." The quote is from Kofi Annan, the United Nation's seventh (coincidence? I think not) secretary general and the first African American to hold that position. It's nice to know that even though we don't know who they are, the Sevens seem to have the back of the community, in a variety of ways.

*The University of Virginia campus is always referred to as Grounds.

SECRET SOCIETIES AT UVA

WHAT: Underground clubs that are active at the University of Virginia

WHERE: The Rotunda is at 1826 University Ave.

COST: Free, but if you're a member, philanthropy is clearly a requirement.

PRO TIP: Leave a note at the Jefferson Statue, thanking the Seven Society for their support of the community.

THE CENTRAL EYESORE

What's the deal with the 11-story concrete skeleton on the Downtown Mall?

In the middle of Charlottesville's crown jewel, the downtown pedestrian mall, sits the area's biggest eyesore. Some call it the Landmark, but its current owner, John Dewberry, calls it Dewberry Living. The unfinished property has been sitting in its present condition since 2009. Plans exist to develop the property into high-end apartments, but a long saga of disputes over parking, tax breaks, and zoning requirements have created a stalemate between the owner and the city. In 2019, the city requested via certified letter permission to inspect the structural integrity of the structure; permission was denied.

Without windows, elevators, railings, or any buildout beyond its concrete and steel frame, Dewberry is home to graffiti on its boarded-up main floor, and provides shelter with its façade overhang.

The unoccupied building provides shelter for rodents, as well, with several reports of rat sightings from downtown business owners and visitors, citing the Landmark specifically.

In 2015, city council candidate Mike Signer vowed in his campaign to explore all legal actions to rid the downtown area of the eyesore. Signer went on to serve as mayor of Charlottesville from 2016 to 2018, a term that bookended the area's 2017 Summer of Hate and the Unite the Right rally that culminated

DOWNTOWN CONCRETE SKELETON

WHAT: The abandoned construction site on the Downtown Mall

WHERE: Corner of 2nd St. and East Main

COST: Free

PRO TIP: On windy days, steer clear of the building—sometimes debris comes loose and falls to the ground.

A luxury hotel and then apartments were planned for the location, but currently no one knows what will become of the Dewberry-owned property, or when construction will resume.

in the murder of Heather Heyer. And yet, the eyesore remains, unaltered except for weather-related wear and tear.

Newcomers may think they're seeing a construction project in progress. Upon closer inspection, most must realize that what they're seeing is a dead-in-the-water development, with no firm plans for change.

Making lemonade out of lemons, local artist Jeff Debrow has used the structure as a canvas for innovative and engaging light shows, sharing his creative artwork in way that delights passers-by. The Charlottesville Mural Project also has used the site to display works of art along the construction fence that borders one side of the building.

DEAD POET SOCIETY

Does this dorm room seem haunted to you?

Edgar Allan Poe slept at the University of Virginia (UVa) as a poverty-stricken student for some months in 1826. You can visit the sealed dorm room on Grounds and listen for the beating of a tell-tale heart. Room No. 13 on the West Range of UVa's historic Lawn, part of Thomas Jefferson's original Academical Village, is outfitted with period furniture, most of which does not have an actual connection to the poet. It is, in fact, not clear whether the room was Poe's actual residence (it may have been No. 17, which has a similar view), but it is known that Poe stayed in one of the West Range rooms a short distance from the Rotunda. Visitors can listen to an audio recording about the University at the time of Poe's attendance there.

From time to time the University gives tours with guides in Poe-era costumes, and fans have gathered at the site. An exhibit of Poe artifacts resides in the Albert and Shirley Small Special Collections Library just across the street from the West Range.

EDGAR ALLAN POE'S ROOM

WHAT: Dorm room celebrating Poe's stay at the University of Virginia

WHERE: UVa Grounds, McCormick Rd., West Range, Room #13

COST: Free

PRO TIP: Venture across the street to the Albert and Shirley Small Special Collections Library to see an exhibit of Poe artifacts.

The bed in the room is the one Poe slept in while living with his foster parents in Richmond. Poe's middle name, Allan, comes from the surname of his foster family.

Edgar Allan Poe's room is an easy one to visit on any self-guided tour of UVa.

While other writers have been associated with the University over the years, none have more fame or following than Edgar Allan Poe. The group responsible for the maintenance and promotion of the room is the Raven Society, the oldest and most prestigious honorary society at the University of Virginia. Among other activities, the Raven Society sponsors the Raven Fellowship, a monetary award to undergraduate or graduate students who undertake creative pursuits separate from their course load. We think Poe would approve.

CRASH SITE ON BUCKS ELBOW MOUNTAIN

What really happened to Flight 349?

On October 30, 1959, a DC-3 crashed into Bucks Elbow Mountain near Crozet en route to Charlottesville-Albemarle Airport. Twenty-six of the 27 passengers were killed, making it the only known commercial plane crash with a single survivor. There are several theories about what happened the night of the crash, including the radio signal being overwhelmed by a stronger signal out of an airport in Maryland, the mental health of the pilot, or suboptimal weather conditions. The crash's sole survivor, Phil Bradley, spent more than three days alone on the mountain in the cold and rain with a dislocated hip, surrounded by wreckage and deceased fellow passengers, before a rescue team located the crash and began the mission to transport him to safety and recover the dead.

It's possible to hike to the site today from Mint Springs Park, a six-mile round-trip hike that has some significant elevation. If you can get permission from the landowners, there's a shorter hike from the top of the mountain, but the site is gated and locked. A memorial to the crew and passengers who perished in the crash is at the base

MEMORIAL OF FLIGHT 349

WHAT: Site and memorial of the plane crash of Piedmont Flight 349

WHERE: Bucks Elbow Mountain and Mint Springs Valley Park, Crozet, VA

COST: Free

PRO TIP: Trespassing is illegal, so take care to obey signs marking private property. Mint Springs Valley Park offers hiking trails, fishing, and swimming in season, so prepare to take full advantage of the park when you visit.

Pay your respects to the souls lost on Flight 349 at the base of Bucks Elbow Mountain, at the memorial in Mint Springs Park.

IN REMEMBRANCE
DEDICATED OCT. 2, 1999
THIS MEMORIAL WAS DESIGNED, BUILT
AND DEDICATED BY THE SOLE SURVIVOR,
E. PHIL BRADLEY, IN THE CRASH OF
PIEDMONT AIRLINE FLIGHT #349 ON
OCTOBER 30, 1959 IN MEMORY OF THE
TWENTY-SIX DISTINGUISHED BUSINESS
MEN AND WOMEN WHO LOST THEIR LIVES.

of the mountain in Mint Springs Park and has the name of each engraved in granite. Visitors can easily see the memorial and take a hike at least partway up the mountain, reflecting on the legacy of a sole survivor, and of the lives lost so long ago.

Phil Bradley wrote a book about his experience: *Sole Survivor: The Crash of Piedmont Flight 349 into Bucks Elbow Mt. As Told By the Sole Survivor, E. Philip Bradley,* which is available via Amazon. Bradley died in 2013 at the age of 87.

HOME TO THE GRAND DUCHESS OF RUSSIA

Was Anna Anderson the real Anastasia?

From 1968 until her death in 1984, Anastasia, the grand duchess of Russia and the sole survivor of the Romanov family, lived in Charlottesville.

Sound improbable?

What's true is that a woman who went by the name Anna Anderson lived and died in Charlottesville, and believed that she was Anastasia. Her claims were disproven by mitochondrial DNA testing done after the fall of the Soviet Union, when the remains of all the Romanovs were located, but that didn't happen until 2007.

It's a tale that's sad, romantic, and strange. Anna Anderson came to Charlottesville via a sponsor in 1968. Gleb Botkin was the son of the Romanov family's personal physician, Dr. Yevgeny Botkin. Dr. Botkin was murdered by the Bolsheviks alongside the Tsar and his family. Gleb Botkin told his friend, history professor and genealogist John Eacott "Jack" Manahan, about the woman he believed was Anastasia, and Manahan paid for Anderson's journey to the United States.

Manahan, a wealthy professor at the University of Virginia, sponsored Anna, and at the end of her six-month visa, married her. The couple lived at 35 University Circle and were well-known in the town as eccentrics.

ANASTASIA IN CHARLOTTESVILLE

WHAT: Home of the woman many thought was Anastasia Romanov

WHERE: 35 University Cir.

COST: Swing by Barracks Rd. and get a coffee at Greenberry's for about $3.

NOTEWORTHY: After the Romanov burial site was discovered and DNA testing completed, the remains of the Romanov family, including Anastasia, were reinterred in Saint Petersburg, Russia, in 1998.

The homes around University Circle were once (and are often still) occupied by UVa faculty. Many are fine, historic properties and others are rentals filled with students, fraternities, and sororities.

Their home, despite their wealth, was in a perpetual state of decline, filled with dogs, cats, and bags of garbage. Anna's health declined in her later years, and after one long hospital stay, Manahan sidestepped a medical release from the doctors and kidnapped his wife. He then took Anna on a wild, slow-speed excursion during which they lived out of their station wagon for a few days. Anna died of pneumonia shortly thereafter, at the age of 88.

There have been many Anastasia impostors from the time the Romanov family was killed until their remains were scientifically verified through DNA testing in 2007, but Anna Anderson was by far the most famous and, around Charlottesville at least, the most widely accepted as the real deal.

Barracks Road Shopping Center was once home to an all-you-can-eat cafeteria with low prices, a favorite of university students. It wasn't uncommon to see Anna Anderson, surrounded by shopping bags, stationed at a table in a corner, enjoying a meal.

ART AND POETRY ON THE CORNER

Can you find the mural inspired by the poet Rita Dove?

Stretching high above University Avenue is a colorful mural painted on the side of the Graduate Hotel building. Visible from the Grounds of the University of Virginia, the mural includes Rita Dove's poem, "Testimonial," from her book of poems, *On the Bus with Rosa Parks.*

"The world called and I answered," reads a line from the poem and the centerpiece of the mural, providing an inspirational message to all who see it.

Dove is the Henry Hoyns Professor of Creative Writing at UVa and a Charlottesville resident. She also was the poet laureate of the United States under President Barack Obama and the Poet Laureate of the Commonwealth of Virginia. She was the first African American Poet Laureate Consultant in Poetry appointed to the Library of Congress. Dove has won numerous awards, among them a Pulitzer Prize in poetry. She is one of the most lauded of Charlottesville's residents.

Muralist David Guinn was commissioned to create the piece using Dove's poetry, with support from the University's Office of the Provost and the Vice Provost for the Arts, the Charlottesville Mural Project, and New City Arts.

RITA DOVE MURAL

WHAT: A mural by David Guinn celebrating the poem "Testimonial," by Rita Dove.

WHERE: The Graduate Hotel, 1309 W. Main St.

COST: Free

PRO TIP: After admiring the mural, zip up to the rooftop bar of the Graduate for a craft cocktail and amazing views.

Full of shops, restaurants, and bars, the Corner is a popular destination for students and community members. Try a Gus Burger at the White Spot while you're there.

When visiting the Corner, the dining and shopping district near the grounds of UVa, it's easy to see how the eye can be drawn to the bright yellow, blue, and white above the 14th Street train trestle. It's a lovely, inspiring sight, especially on a gray, overcast day.

Rita Dove herself took up paint and brush to add the finishing touches to the mural, at the artist's invitation.

JAZZ FOR CHARITY

What's an inexpensive way to wow your date for Valentine's Day?

It's often a struggle to find that winning combination of fun and affordability for Valentine's Day. One community event is a solid choice every year. For the $5 per person admission to the Jefferson Theater, guests are treated to a fantastic night of jazz and swing. The event raises money for the band—the award-winning jazz band from Albemarle High School, which is fronted by vocalists from the school's equally talented choral program. Special guests from Charlottesville's community of famed musicians sometimes sit in, including John D'earth, Charles Owens, and Terri Allard.

D'earth is the Director of Jazz Performance at the University of Virginia as well as the artist in residence at Virginia Commonwealth University. He has played with Miles Davis, the Dave Matthews Band, and Buddy Rich.

STAR-POWERED JAZZ

WHAT: Community jazz dance

WHERE: Jefferson Theater, 110 E. Main St.

COST: $5 per person

PRO TIP: Grab tacos or nachos for dinner at the adjacent Cinema Taco before the dance.

John D'earth is a regular feature at Miller's, a stone's throw from the Jefferson Theater. You can catch him there for late-night performances. And once in a blue moon, he'll surprise locals by appearing as the most talented busker on the Downtown Mall.

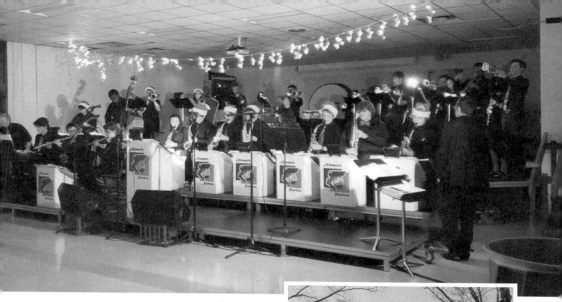

With an orchestra, marching band, pep band, and jazz band, the music program at Albemarle High School is active and very strong! Photos courtesy of AHS Jazz Band

Because of the excellence of the high school student musicians and the star-power the event attracts, community members of all ages flock to the dance, where they can cut the rug to jazz and other music, as the band uses this chance to flex its skills with pop and R&B tunes to delight the audience.

Greg Thomas, the now-retired, longtime band director at Albemarle High School, founded the Jazz Band Dance and has been instrumental in its ongoing success.

Proceeds raised at the dance help pay for the students to travel to competitions.

NATURE, PLAY, AND DISCOVERY

Where does mental health meet the great outdoors?

The mental health benefits of being outside in nature are well-known. Childhood development benefits from connecting with nature as well. Wildrock, a three-and-a-half-acre property developed with psychology and mental health in mind, is an outdoor play, discovery, and retreat center. Wildrock was created by countless volunteers and community partners. From Sally Mander, a one-of-a-kind piece created on-site by an artisan, to the Nest, created and maintained by several volunteer groups over the years, to the crafted play materials throughout the playscape and Discovery Barn, visitors have an experience at Wildrock that they truly can't find anywhere else.

Located adjacent to the Patricia Ann Byrom Forest Preserve, the largest park in Albemarle County, the playscape features a stream and pastures framed by mountains in the distance. There's a barn and a hobbit house for indoor exploration and a walking labyrinth to traverse.

Families and children's groups have begun to discover this treasure, and more recently nonprofit groups and human service workers are beginning to take advantage of customized retreats that get teams into the outdoors to learn and develop stronger relationships.

Because it's not always possible for children to get to Wildrock, the program has partnered with Charlottesville City

---

Local construction nonprofit Building Goodness Foundation has contributed the time of skilled volunteers to design and build structures for play at Wildrock.

Kids, parents, and community members enjoy all that Wildrock has to offer. With its beautiful surroundings, Wildrock is an excellent place to explore, stretch, and learn. Photos courtesy of Wildrock.

NATURE PLAYSCAPE

WHAT: Wildrock outdoor play area

WHERE: 6600 Blackwells Hollow Rd., Crozet, VA

COST: $20 visits, $395 summer camps

PRO TIP: Finding Wildrock can be tricky. GPS is not reliable and may incorrectly lead to Cottonwood Headquarters Rd. Follow the directions on Wildrock's website and stay on Rte. 810 until you reach the black pasture fence and gravel drive.

Schools to bring a little bit of nature to the kids. Traveling outreach programs provide after-school activities, therapeutic nature play, and themed pop-up programs that delve deeper into art, literature, and science-themed learning.

Some lucky kids know that Wildrock also is a great place to host a birthday party. Parents like it because the cleanup is easy when everything is outdoors!

Make a reservation to take your family—or all the neighborhood kids—and play alongside them, discovering nature right in our backyard.

A SECRET ROSE GARDEN

Where does it rain rose petals?

New Dominion Bookshop is the oldest bookstore in the commonwealth of Virginia and is known for its exemplary customer service and cozy atmosphere. A grand staircase leads to a second-story stage, perfect for small author events, readings, and book clubs. The light streaming in from the second-floor windows creates an excellent atmosphere for browsing. With more than 20,000 books in the shop, there's a good read for every taste.

The secret about the shop is what lies behind it. Through the store and out the back door, guests will find a glorious secret rose garden, walled in by the brick buildings on either side and a fence protecting it from the street beyond. In the springtime, the blooms fill an archway above, and guests are permitted to bring a lunch and sit among the rose petals.

Carol Troxell, the bookshop's former owner, planted the garden off the Fourth Street alleyway, and staff at the shop and a local volunteer care for the blooms.

THE BOOKSHOP ROSE GARDEN

WHAT: The hidden rose garden behind New Dominion Bookshop

WHERE: 404 E. Main St.

COST: Buy a book while you're in the shop! How can you resist?

PRO TIP: Best-selling author John Grisham, a Charlottesville resident and man-about-town, debuts his novels at the store, and signed copies of new editions are often available.

A local physician volunteers his time pruning and looking after the rose garden, which makes these plants some of the best-tended in town.

Tear yourself away from the beauty and solitude of the hidden rose garden to browse and buy in the bookstore.

Follow the bookshop online to stay alert to Rose Garden Days, when you can plan to sit below the blooms and read an English romance novel or a book of poetry. Looking for a special tiny wedding venue for you and your beloved fellow bookhound? This garden is open to event bookings.

DISCOVER LATIN SOCIAL DANCING

Do you know how to salsa or bachata?

Edwin Roa is the founder of Zabor Dance and the instigator behind Charlottesville Salsa Club. To generate interest from beginners, Edwin began hosting two weekly parties; Sundays are for salsa, and Wednesdays are for bachata fusion. Bachata, which originated in the 1950s in the Dominican Republic, is a sensual dance that has gone mainstream. It is slower than salsa, and similar to bolero and merengue.

The club starts each party with a lesson, making sure the environment is welcoming for all beginners. Then the more seasoned dancers hit their stride and really show off their moves. Come as a spectator and you may find that your feet make the decision to join in for you!

DANCE PARTY

WHAT: Salsa and bachata nights

WHERE: IX Art Park

COST: Free

PRO TIP: Wear shoes that fit well and clothes that move with you for the most comfortable dance experience.

TV shows like *So You Think You Can Dance* and *Dancing with the Stars* have helped fuel interest in dance parties and competitions, even in Charlottesville.

Fun, family-friendly IX Art Park is a great setting for outdoor, group dance instruction and a great way to get a workout. Photos courtesy of Zabor Dance.

The dance parties are welcoming and inclusive for all. Many dancers bring their children, and people of all ages enjoy the events.

If the salsa club dance parties really pique your interest, sign up for regular lessons through Zabor Dance, and get ready to sweep local competitions.

A CONGREGATION WITH HISTORY

How can you get a benediction for your dog?

One of the oldest churches in the area, Grace Episcopal Church in Keswick, is in fact one of six congregations that have been active since Virginia was a colony. Built in 1745, the church and its grounds have much to offer guests.

For those interested in the rich history of the region, the church grounds feature a large graveyard where members of Virginia's oldest families are interred. There are 110 known veterans from the Civil War through the Vietnam War buried there, and the church provides a guide to allow visitors to pay their respects.

The church was designed in the Gothic Revival style originally by the architect William Strickland. It partially burned and was rebuilt in 1895, with a parish hall and other buildings added over the years. The 1,575-pound bell in the church tower is original and is still in use.

Stained glass enthusiasts will enjoy the view of six Tiffany-inspired windows, each of which tells a visual story about the benefactor who donated it to the church.

WHERE HISTORY LIVES

WHAT: Grace Episcopal Church and Graveyard

WHERE: 5607 Gordonsville Rd., #43, Keswick, VA

COST: Donations requested

NOTABLE: Motivated by the tragic and historic events that occurred in Charlottesville in 2017, members of the congregation resolved to acknowledge the past and enhance their knowledge of local racial history. The African American History Project (AAHP) began with a small committee of church and community members researching books and documents and collecting oral histories to take a deeper look at connections to the local Black community and churches.

The drive out to Grace Episcopal Church is as scenic as the destination, with rolling horse farms on either side. The graveyard itself is a lovely, well-maintained memorial that spans several acres.

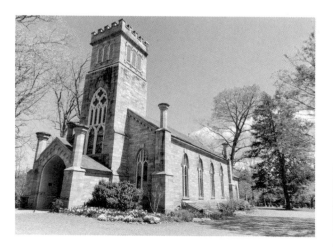

But Grace Episcopal is most fondly known for an annual event held every Thanksgiving Day. The first Blessing of the Hounds ceremony was in 1929, and the tradition has continued uninterrupted ever since. Fox hunters astride their horses and decked out in red coats gather with their trusty hounds for a special prayer and ceremony. Well-behaved dogs and their owners are welcome to attend and receive the annual benediction. A collection is taken and proceeds go to area nonprofits such as Service Dogs of Virginia and The Wildlife Center of Virginia.

Grace Episcopal is, above all, a church with a diverse congregation. All who are sincerely interested in the worship of God, and the enjoyment of great music, fellowship, and Christian formation are invited to attend.

Grace Church architect William Strickland (1788–1854) was well-known for many buildings he designed in Philadelphia, Pennsylvania, and also in Nashville, Tennessee. Grace Church is his only work in Virginia.

BLESSED BE THE CHEESE

Where can you find some holy cheese?

A short drive into the country can bring you to Our Lady of the Angels, a Trappist monastery run by a group of nuns. These enterprising sisters combine prayer and hard work, raising and caring for dairy cows and producing fresh cheese sold to visitors, local stores, and restaurants.

The cheese-making business has sustained the order since 1990. The nuns use techniques developed in the Netherlands to produce a semi-soft, mild, Dutch-style Gouda cheese from the milk produced by their dairy cows. The two-pound wheels are coated in red wax, and the sisters sell them for $25, cash only, on-site. The cheese is delicious; worth every penny, and the scenic journey to get it makes it even better.

While you're there, explore the chapel and pause for some prayer or meditation in the pastoral Virginia countryside.

After your visit to the monastery, if you like a little wine with your cheese, head to the nearby White Hall Winery for a picnic.

THE BEST GOUDA CHEESE

WHAT: Our Lady of the Angels Monastery

WHERE: 3365 Monastery Dr., Crozet, VA

COST: $25

PRO TIP: Put your uncut wheel in the back of your fridge for a year to let it age in cave-like conditions. The result is a deeper, more intense flavor and is totally worth the wait.

Top: *The view from the monastery.* Bottom left: *A stained-glass window.*
Bottom right: *A wheel of gouda made by the nuns. Photo by Jennifer Brecht.*

Americans typically pronounce the name of the
cheese the nuns sell as "goo-dah," but the proper
pronunciation of the Dutch cheese sounds a little
more like "how-dah," although your cheesemonger
might be surprised to hear you ask for gouda as
though you're from the Netherlands.

MARKED BY THESE MONUMENTS

What will be the fate of monuments to hate?

Monuments to the Confederacy and symbols of hate are, in decreasing number, sprinkled throughout the South. Until July of 2021, the city of Charlottesville was home to Confederate statues, including the Robert E. Lee, Stonewall Jackson, and the Johnny Reb statues. A statue of George Rogers Clark stood near the corner of the Grounds at the University of Virginia, and a statue of Lewis, Clark, and Sacagawea was at the corner of West Main and McIntire. Four statues, Clark, Lee, Jackson, and Lewis and Clark were removed in a single weekend in July, 2021 and are in storage, awaiting their fates.

It had been an active era for the monuments. Renewed interest began in February 2017, as part of a movement started by high school student Zyahna Bryant in 2016 to take down the three Confederate statues. City Council members voted three to two to take down the Robert E. Lee statue and rename Lee Park. It turned out that it wasn't as easy as all that, and a string of lawsuits and court injunctions delayed the removal, with the case going all the way to the Virginia Supreme Court.

Other racist monuments and memorials are being changed. The UVa Board of Visitors voted to rededicate or move the "Whispering Wall," a memorial to Confederate soldier Frank Hume, and to rename Withers-Brown Hall and the Curry School of Education. J. L. M. Curry and Henry Malcolm Withers, neither of whom attended or worked at UVA, were known segregationists.

The statues of Robert E. Lee (left), Stonewall Jackson (center), and George Rogers Clark (right) were removed in July, 2021.

One statue was removed before the others. Johnny Reb, formally called *At Ready*, was a monument paid for by the Daughters of the Confederacy and dedicated in 1909. The statue of a Confederate soldier and his cannons was removed from its spot in front of the Albemarle County courthouse in downtown Charlottesville in September 2020. Dr. Andrea Douglas, executive director of the Jefferson School African American Heritage Center, and Dr. Jalane Schmidt, associate professor of religious studies at UVa, offer informational walking tours of the area, including the site of the Slave Auction Block Marker, a monument repeatedly stolen and replaced in the Court Square area of downtown Charlottesville. A virtual version of the tour lives at www.thesemonuments.org, presented by WTJU-91.9 FM.

UNWANTED MONUMENTS

WHAT: Confederate statues and monuments to racism

WHERE: Market Street Park, Court Square Park, downtown, and UVa Grounds

COST: Free

NOTABLE: The controversy over removing the statues attracted white supremacists to hold the Unite the Right rally in Charlottesville, where one person was killed and dozens injured, bringing worldwide attention to the city.

RARE ART COLLECTION

Why is a world-class museum of indigenous Australian art in Charlottesville?

Visitors to Charlottesville are surprised to learn that the city is home to one of the finest collections of Australian Aboriginal art in the world. The museum, called the Kluge-Ruhe Aboriginal Art Collection, is a unit of the University of Virginia and is named after the two collections that are the basis of the museum's permanent holdings. It is the only museum outside of Australia dedicated to indigenous Australian art.

Australian Aboriginal culture is the oldest continuous tradition on the planet. The culture dates back 80,000 years, when people first settled in Australia. Still-visible rock art dates back 20,000 years. Indigenous Australian artists have continued their tradition, and the museum has works that span ancient to contemporary art.

How did this museum in Charlottesville, a collection so highly regarded that it rivals museums in Australia, come to be? Kluge-Ruhe is named for its collectors. John Kluge was an early media mogul, making his billions founding Metromedia, the precursor to the Fox news network. In 1988, Kluge attended an exhibition called *Dreamings: The Art of Aboriginal Australia*, at the Asia Society Galleries in New York City. Moved by the art he saw there, Kluge at once became an avid collector. In 1993, Kluge acquired the collection of the late Edward Ruhe (1923–1989), an English professor at the University of Kansas who began collecting Aboriginal art in 1965 while in Australia as a Fulbright

John Kluge's third wife, Patricia Kluge, kept the couple's Albemarle estate after their divorce. That property was sold in 2011 and is now known as Trump Winery.

The art collection is housed in this beautiful, large building on a former farm on Pantops Mountain, now owned by the University of Virginia.

ABORIGINAL ART COLLECTION

WHAT: The Kluge-Ruhe Aboriginal Art Collection

WHERE: 400 Worrell Dr.

COST: Free

PRO TIP: The grounds around the building are lovely, and there are paved walking trails with ponds and occasional sculptures nearby. If weather permits, plan to take a long outdoor stroll.

Visiting Professor. Ruhe was the first person in the United States to exhibit a privately owned collection of Aboriginal art.

Kluge donated the collection for scholarly research to the University of Virginia in 1997 and the museum opened its location on Pantops Farm, property once owned by Thomas Jefferson, east of the city of Charlottesville in Albemarle County. Today, the museum has a collection of more than 2,100 pieces.

For those who can't visit the museum in person, the entire collection is now online, where visitors can explore paintings, glassworks, fiber works, photography, sculptures, prints, drawings, and other works. Virtual tours, lectures, teaching tools, and a kit for kids and families to access the museum are also available.

HELP FROM HOLLYWOOD

How did a Hollywood director come to create a resource for the homeless?

The Haven's entire mission is to end homelessness in Charlottesville. Founded through the generosity of a Hollywood director, Tom Shadyac, the shelter and resource for those seeking stable housing opened its doors near the Downtown Mall in 2010.

Fostering a culture of "radical hospitality," The Haven's executive director, Stephen Hitchcock, says that the organization strives to make homelessness a rare, brief, and non-recurring event.

In its more than 10 years of operation, the organization has seen some success, with chronic homelessness reduced by 65% in the region. Operating a day shelter is only part of what the organization does. Connection to housing case managers and other critical resources that aim to reduce the need for The Haven to operate, makes up the remainder of its offerings.

The shelter is housed in a building once used as a church, which means that it includes not only beautiful chapel space—providing a quiet place for reflection and prayer—but also an attractive space the community can reserve for weddings and events, providing

Weekly, the kitchen opens to the community for The Haven Homecooking. For a $10 donation, anyone can come and enjoy an excellent hot meal. The donation helps support guests of the day shelter and provides an opportunity for the guests to work at the lunch café and congregate with members of the community at large. Guest chefs and excellent home cooks volunteer their time, providing a tasty, rotating menu that makes The Haven one of the hottest lunch tickets in town.

The beautiful chapel at The Haven is the scene of many weddings, and is especially attractive for its proximity to the Downtown Mall.

THE HAVEN

WHAT: A day shelter and resource for homeless guests

WHERE: 112 W. Market St.

COST: Lunch at The Haven is a $10 donation.

PRO TIP: Check The Haven's Homecooking Facebook page to see the featured chef and lunch menu for the week.

ongoing income to help sustain the nonprofit.

But how the heck did Hollywood make The Haven happen? University of Virginia graduate Tom Shadyac was once known as the youngest-ever joke writer for Bob Hope. The director, screenwriter, producer, and author has *Ace Ventura: Pet Detective*, *Bruce Almighty*, *The Nutty Professor*, and *Patch Adams* on his resume. In 2005, Tom returned to central Virginia to film the sequel to *Bruce Almighty*, the movie *Evan Almighty*, in a field that is now the Crozet neighborhood of Old Trail. While the crew members were in town, they became acquainted with some of Charlottesville's population of unhoused people, and Tom was moved to do something to help.

Tom bought and renovated the historic First Christian Church at First and Market in the heart of Charlottesville with the purpose of creating a day shelter and social resource center. His vision became reality, and The Haven now thrives as an independent nonprofit, working hard to make itself obsolete as it strives to end homelessness in the community.

DAVE MATTHEWS BAND TOUR

Will you march in Dave's steps?

Fans of Dave Matthews and the Dave Matthews Band (DMB) know that Charlottesville is where Dave got his start. Most find their way to Miller's, a bar and pool hall on the Downtown Pedestrian Mall, to pay homage to the place where their hero used to tend bar. Miller's is still a popular music venue and watering hole, so it's an easy part of the DMB pilgrimage.

The rest of the tour, however, includes some more obscure but notable stops. Take a walk around the Rose Hill neighborhood where Dave's bandmates, Carter Beauford, LeRoi Moore, and Boyd Tinsley, all grew up.

The Music Resource Center, located in a renovated church at 105 Ridge Street provides music lessons and recording equipment through a nonprofit funded by DMB and serves kids in sixth to 12th grade.

On South Street downtown, a three-story pink building is part of a common Charlottesville skyline image. Called the Pink Warehouse, its greatest claim to fame in this storyline is that its rooftop was the site of the first-ever Dave Matthews Band concert. If you were there, good for you. You're in select company.

WALK WHERE DAVE WALKED

WHAT: A tour of Dave Matthews Band-related sights

WHERE: Various spots around town

COST: Free

PRO TIP: Ask a local to share their "Dave" connection or sighting story. They might even have a photo on their phone.

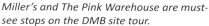
Miller's and The Pink Warehouse are must-see stops on the DMB site tour.

Booker T. Washington Park's playground and picnic shelter were donated by the band.

Travel up north on Route 29 to visit Holly Memorial Gardens; LeRoi is buried there.

Head out to the country to visit Blenheim Vineyards, the winery owned and designed by Dave Matthews.

But most of all, keep your eyes open at all times, as when Dave is in town, you might see him shopping, walking downtown, or stopping for a cup of coffee.

When white supremacists descended upon Charlottesville in the summer of 2017, DMB coordinated the Concert for Charlottesville at Scott Stadium, raising money to help those healing from the violence and hate.

A MEMORIAL TO JOHN HENRY JAMES

What happened at Wood's Crossing?

In 1898, as 20-year-old Julia Hotopp returned from a trip into Charlottesville to her home in what is now Pen Park, she was violently attacked. Her brother, Carl, found her unconscious.

John Henry James was an African American man, living in Charlottesville and working odd jobs. Just after the crime was reported, James was found at a nearby saloon. The authorities determined that James fit the description offered by Miss Hotopp and he was accused of a violent sexual assault and detained. There were details that did not fit, but the authorities persisted. The accused was transported by train to a jail in Staunton, Virginia, and a jury assembled the very next day.

James was found guilty, and officers accompanied him on the train back to Charlottesville for sentencing. When the train pulled into the stop at Wood's Crossing, they were greeted by a mob of between 100 and 150 white men who demanded James be handed over to them. Despite James's claim of innocence and the lack of evidence of his guilt, the mob hanged him there that day, and then riddled his body with 30 bullets.

Wood's Crossing is on land that is now Farmington Country Club.

COMMUNITY REMEMBRANCE PROJECT

WHAT: John Henry James Memorial

WHERE: Albemarle County Office Building, 401 McIntire Rd.

COST: Free

PRO TIP: The members of the lynch mob did not bother to conceal their identities, yet no one was ever charged with the killing. The only known participant was Carl Hotopp, Julia's brother.

Left: *Soil from the site of the lynching of John Henry James is kept as a memorial in the Albemarle County Courthouse. Photo by Mike Kropf.* Right: *Outside, a marker tells the story.*

In July, 2018, nearly 120 years later, a group of local activists met on the grounds of the private golf community to gather at the lynching site and hold a memorial service for James. The Charlottesville mayor, members of the clergy, descendants of people enslaved in the community, and racial justice activists attended the service. Three containers were filled with soil: one for the City of Charlottesville, one for Albemarle County. The third container was installed as part of an exhibit containing collections of soil from lynching sites at the Equal Justice Initiative's National Memorial for Peace and Justice in Montgomery, Alabama. An exhibit on James is in the Albemarle County Office Building and includes the glass jar of soil for the County.

Most current residents never knew about the lynching or this part of Charlottesville's history until intrepid historians tracked down and publicized the story and the search for the location of the event, in an effort to memorialize and honor the memory of the deceased.

Julia's father was William Friedrich Hotopp, the founder of the Monticello Wine Company, the headquarters of which stood on Charlottesville's north side, with the manager living on what is still known as Wine Street. Hotopp also managed the Woolen Mills and built the city's Jefferson Theater.

FROM GARDEN TO GLASS

Where can you find homebrew supplies and more?

The unassuming shop sits back from the road at 900 Preston Avenue. Its storefront windows and large garage door suggest something more industrial than retail. Gardeners, homebrewers, and fans of other DIY pursuits know the secret. Behind the front retail space of the shop exists the largest Fifth Season location, with more than 1,200 square feet. Fifth Season has four locations in North Carolina and its flagship in good old Charlottesville, Virginia. Visitors find everything an aspiring organic gardener might need. Known for homebrew supplies, the store is invested in nurturing the brewing community, brewing in-house specialty beers in support of community efforts, and offering guidance to the uninitiated.

GARDEN AND BREWING SUPPLY STORE

WHAT: Fifth Season

WHERE: 900 Preston Ave.

COST: Browsing is free, retail prices vary

PRO TIP: Follow the Fifth Season blog for great tips on better homebrewing and organic gardening.

Master gardeners offer classes in the store's vast gathering space. A collection of pots, stone statues, bird feeders, and other garden accoutrements are also available for sale.

Interested in learning to can, preserve, or make your own cheese? They have starter kits and supplies for these pursuits, as well.

Fifth Season's in-house craft brewery hosts tastings and beer sales in its tiny parking lot beer garden.

Fifth Season offers garden supplies, homebrew and hydroponics equipment, a brewery, and a tasting room and patio.

How about hydroponics? For the urban gardener, or year-round home farmer, this method of indoor plant nurturing might be just the ticket.

Fifth Season is a good place to get your kids interested in gardens, as well. There are supplies for creating fairy gardens, as well as an excellent array of houseplants to give as gifts or to turn your indoor environment green.

CATCH A CONCERT

Why not sample a show before you buy?

That white, mushroom-like tent at the east end of the Downtown Mall plays host to most of Charlottesville's large concerts when the weather is nice enough for outdoor shows. There are many seats under the tent, and further back there are general admission seats for those who want to lounge on a patch of grass as they listen to their favorite bands.

Food trucks, beer, and wine stands are available for ticket holders to enhance their overall experience.

If you're on the fence about the band performing, or have seen them enough that an encore performance isn't in your budget, we suggest an alternative.

Locals in the know will time a dinner date at Himalayan Fusion, the Pavilion's closest restaurant with outdoor seating. You can dine in comfort at your table on the patio and listen to most bands as they perform. You won't be able to see the acts, and much of what's said will be lost on you, but the familiar tunes will reach your ears as you enjoy your dinner.

THE SPRINT PAVILION

WHAT: How to listen to a concert downtown for free

WHERE: 700 E. Main St.

COST: Free

PRO TIP: Food trucks line the Pavilion perimeter on summer Friday evenings, so get outside with the family for an affordable dinner and a show.

Fridays After Five is a series of free concerts in the Pavilion, Fridays during the summer months.

*From free Fridays After Five concerts to eavesdropping from the bridge or nearby restaurants'
outdoor seating, there are several ways to enjoy a concert at the Sprint Pavilion.*

Better yet, go out to Market Street on your left and head further
east, up to Avon Street and the Belmont Bridge that stretches up,
over, and behind the Pavilion. Gaps in the tent will give you small
glimpses of the stage, where you can see the acts from the back
side. The acoustics on the bridge are spot-on, though, with most
shows loud enough to reach your ears if you decide to take a walk
through the nearby Belmont neighborhood.

Other concert freeloaders may crowd the bridge if the band is a
very popular one, so be prepared to jostle for space, and to move
along if the authorities decide it's time to clear the sidewalk.

MICHOACÁN SPECIALTIES

Where can you surprise your palate with food from Michoacán, Mexico?

In some parts of the world, people use the term La Michoacana as a catchall to mean ice cream shop, much like we use the word Kleenex for tissues. In fact, there may be up to 30,000 ice cream businesses in Mexico alone that use Michoacana in their name.

In tiny Charlottesville there are two Michoacanas; La Flor Michoacana and La Michoacana Taqueria and Restaurant.

La Flor Michoacana is on Cherry Avenue and, as its name might indicate to those familiar with the brand, is a paleteria, or ice cream shop offering homemade ice cream and authentic Mexican paletas. Paletas are popsicles beyond what any traditional American audience is accustomed. If the only popsicle you've ever had is the sugar water variety that comes wrapped in bright colored paper or plastic (or, heaven forbid, the ghastly ice pop kind), you deserve to try something completely different. Paletas are gorgeous works of art using fresh fruits, cream, and fruit juices. The flavors are beyond comparison. Visitors have

---

LA FLOR MICHOACANA AND LA MICHOACÁN TAQUERIA

WHAT: Michoacán restaurants

WHERE: La Flor Michoacana, 601A Cherry Ave.; La Michoacana Taqueria and Restaurant, 1138 E. High St.

COST: A paleta will run you $3

PRO TIP: Step out of your comfort zone and try new ice cream flavors like Thai tea or guava!

Is a piñata the right activity for your next soirée? The piñata selection at La Flor Michoacana is second to none.

Enjoy a paleta from La Flor Michoacana, shop for candy and pinatas, or enjoy taco Tuesday at La Michoacana restaurant.

difficulty choosing from flavors like yellow cherry, cream cheese, guava, mango chili, tres leches cake, and many more. The ice cream flavors also go far beyond what you'll find among the tired 31.

The first paleterias were started in Tocumbo, Michoacán, Mexico in 1946 by two brothers and their friend. The logo of the little girl in traditional dress has become the ubiquitous symbol of the paleteria, and Charlottesville's La Flor Michoacana sticks to tradition in name, logo, and recipes.

La Michoacana Taqueria and Restaurant is not, however, a paleteria, as the full name indicates. Its menu also is Michoacan Mexican food, and guests will find excellent authentic tacos, fajitas, enchiladas, and more. Located in the Free Bridge neighborhood, the restaurant is tiny and best suited to takeout. Catering also is available.

A BARN UNDER A BRIDGE

Where can you find a better burrito?

It's small, it's simple, it's hard to find . . . it's Barbie's Burrito Barn. Tucked in a small stone cottage under an overpass next to the barn-like building that houses Beck Cohen Heating and Air Conditioning is a Charlottesville favorite. Barbie's offers a menu of California–Mexican fare, great for takeout, available to cater your next event, and just right for an easy, affordable lunch or dinner. Chief cook and bottle-washer Barbie Brannock will make your food and take your order, too.

CALI-MEX FARE

WHAT: Barbie's Burrito Barn

WHERE: 201 Avon St.

COST: $8 and up

PRO TIP: Order an extra side of the crispy strips to dip in salsa or guacamole.

Barbie's menu stands apart as a healthful alternative, with lots of vegetables and her signature crispy tortilla strips.

It's a sweet little secret spot under the bridge. With a handful of outdoor picnic tables and not much more indoor seating, it's perfect for an inexpensive date night or grabbing lunch with a friend. There are a few notable Mexican

Barbie uses lots of fresh vegetables not usually found in Mexican fare. Cabbage, jicama, and radishes play a role, and when ingredients run out, those menu items are gone for the day.

Barbie's Burrito Barn is nearly under the Belmont Bridge, next to the Beck Cohen building and in close proximity to Champion Brewing Company and the Sprint Pavilion.

restaurants in town including Bebedero, La Michoacana, and Conmole, all worth multiple visits. Barbie's though, fills a niche otherwise unfulfilled. If you're in the mood for a light lunch or dinner, and a quick way to get your daily dose of veggies, this is the menu for you.

If you get a chance to visit the loo, don't be surprised to find a full bathtub in there; the space Barbie's occupies was once used as a pet grooming shop.

LARP AT DARDEN TOWE PARK

Do you crave combat?

Live Action Role Playing, otherwise known as LARP, is known to a small subsection of people who are enthusiastic about outdoor recreation, storytelling, and, yes, combat. In Charlottesville, that group is Zorn Vongal, a family-focused battle game in the dark-age, medieval style. Think of the J. R. R. Tolkien Lord of the Rings trilogy come to life.

Zorn Vongal is a member organization with about 40 participants engaging in full-contact combat with buffer weapons. Every Sunday, the group hosts battle and training exercises at Darden Towe Park from noon until around 5 p.m.

The battles are not for the faint of heart, with fiberglass weapons buffered with foam and fabric to cause only minor damage—bruises, but no broken bones or skin. That being said, the organization is focused on health and safety, while providing physically rigorous activity that contributes to storylines and supports mental health. The games focus on honor, integrity, sportsmanship, and teamwork.

Partnered with Living Free, a nonprofit that supports veterans and their children, Zorn Vongal endeavors to teach modern-day chivalry, life lessons, and active therapy to teens

---

What is LARP, anyway? Participants physically portray characters with costumes, names, accents, and behaviors to enact a game plot. Players pursue a goal within a fictional setting and interact with one another in character. LARP can take many different real-world forms.

LARP participants engage in battle at Darden Towe Park. Photos courtesy of Charlottesville Battle Gaming.

ZORN VONGAL

WHAT: Live Action Role Playing

WHERE: 1445 Darden Towe Park

COST: $20/person membership

PRO TIP: If you're brave enough to give battle a try, fill out a waiver (18 and up) and your first practice is free.

and adults who may be dealing with aggression issues, stress, or behavioral problems that come from post-traumatic stress disorder (PTSD) or parents suffering from PTSD.

If participation isn't your bag, Zorn Vongal enthusiastically welcomes spectators, with a painted section marked just for the interested audience. Two special events take place during the year: the Brigand's Ball and the Jilted Lovers' Battle. Both are off-site, extended, weekend-long events, including combat competitions, dancing, singing, a makers' faire, and competitions for sewing and costume creation.

ACKNOWLEDGING HISTORY

Who built the University of Virginia?

For a long time, it seemed like a secret: The University of Virginia was built by enslaved people. The massive undertaking in the 1800s wasn't talked about in this way, and the builders were certainly not honored for their contributions.

A student-led effort to honor the enslaved laborers began in 2010. In 2016, the book, *Mr. Jefferson's University*, developed a plan for a suitable memorial to honor those laborers and craftspeople whose lives were used to create this institution of higher learning.

In 2020, the Memorial to Enslaved Laborers was completed on the grounds of UVa. The structure represents the 4,000 to 5,000 enslaved people who lived and worked at UVa at some point between 1817 and 1865. Each name or listing represents a person who performed a task to build or maintain the university or to serve as students and professors. There were 4,000 known enslaved community members, but full names are known for fewer than 600. Historians continue to work to discover the remaining names to add them to the memorial.

Among the work, enslaved people cleared land, dug foundations, and built all of the buildings—work that included highly skilled labor such as carpentry, brickmaking, roofing, stone carving, blacksmithing, and more. Daily tasks including

---

The University of Virginia is a UNESCO World Heritage Site, a landmark legally protected by the United Nations Educational, Scientific and Cultural Organization. World Heritage Sites are designated for having cultural, historical, scientific, or other significance.

1861
Approximately 14,000 enslaved African Americans, over half the population, live in Albemarle County when the Civil War starts. A half million enslaved people reside in Virginia.

1861
Virginia secedes from the Union, invoking the federal government's "oppression of the slaveholding states."

The Memorial to Enslaved Laborers on the UNESCO Heritage Site at the University of Virginia was dedicated in 2021.

WHAT'S NEW TO SEE AT THE UNIVERSITY OF VIRGINIA?

WHAT: The Memorial to Enslaved Laborers

WHERE: University of Virginia Grounds

COST: Free

PRO TIP: The geometry of the memorial lends itself to an acoustic quality. Listen, and conversations of others within the circle will be clearly audible.

fetching water, chopping and stacking wood, cooking, cleaning, making clothing, and generally seeing to the needs of an entire community fell to these unpaid and mistreated men, women, and children.

The monument is both beautiful and moving, an oasis for peace and reflection. The continued work to add names creates an ever-evolving, continued examination of the true history of the university.

BIKE A MOUNTAIN

Where can beginners and experts ride challenging trails?

In Albemarle County, northeast of Charlottesville, you'll find more than 570 acres of wilderness and trails in Preddy Creek Trail Park. For aspiring mountain bikers, Preddy Creek is ideal. Beginners can start with the Preddy Creek Loop and work their way up. The loop trail offers a smooth tread surface. More advanced riders will enjoy climbs and descents through the trees. Beginner group rides are on Tuesday evenings during Daylight Saving Time, as scheduled through the Charlottesville Area Mountain Bike Club.

An expert loop for seasoned mountain bikers will be opening soon. These trails will offer technical features including log rides, elevated bridges, sweeping berms, rock gardens, and other features.

MOUNTAIN BIKING PARADISE

WHAT: Preddy Creek Trail Park

WHERE: 3690 Burnley Station Rd.

COST: Free

PRO TIP: Check the Charlottesville Area Mountain Bike Club website to learn about races and other special events at Preddy Creek and at other trails in the area.

The Greene County Board of Supervisors has approved development of several homes near Preddy Creek Trail Park, a deal which includes the donation of 50 acres of land adjacent to the park. The county will build a public access trailhead and parking lot and create approximately 10,000 linear feet of trails along Cedar Run and Preddy Creek, beginning sometime in 2023.

Top: *Some trails are easy to moderate, good for kids and families. Photo by Chester Hull.* Inset: *Friends gather to practice advanced mountain biking skills. Photo by Valerie Hill.*

There are 15 or more trails to follow, half at the intermediate level and half at the easy/intermediate level. On a single-wide track, speed can often be what separates the easy from the intermediate. The Advanced Mountain Bike Trail is the only one marked "difficult."

Remember to share, because Preddy Creek isn't just for mountain bikers. Hikers, runners, and even horseback riders will be there to enjoy the trails as well. (No horses are allowed on the Advanced Mountain Bike Trail).

A public park, Preddy Creek opens at 7 a.m. and closes at dusk, so plan your visit accordingly.

WATER THERAPY

Where can you find a refuge for peace and healing downtown?

Alternative healing and stress-reducing activities are more popular than ever, and Charlottesville has many options to suit your needs. But there is only one place where guests can float, gravity-free, in a private tank of warm salt water.

A short downtown walk can get you to a modest building, perhaps not by accident in close proximity to numerous therapists' and doctors' offices. Inside AquaFloat, it's a spa atmosphere. Soft lighting, soothing music, and calming hues greet guests.

A single session will run you $65, but the stress reduction is well worth it. The almost-embryonic sensory deprivation experience is so popular that people sign up for long-term memberships, allowing them to float monthly or even more frequently.

Combine your float with a massage or some time in a sauna, and it's a real spa day outing.

Float fans say that they benefit from reduced pain and stress and that floating helps them achieve a meditative state or increases creativity. Athletes believe that floating helps with muscle recovery.

In the tank, about 12 inches of water and 1,000 pounds of Epsom salts are heated to about 93.5 degrees—about as warm as the temperature of your skin. Close the tank lid and turn off the lights and you could be in outer space for all you know. Leave your worries outside and enjoy the experience for about an hour.

HYDROTHERAPY

WHAT: AquaFloat

WHERE: 925 E. Jefferson St.

COST: $65 and up

PRO TIP: Floating is about relaxing, so to prepare for your float, skip the caffeine for four to six hours in advance.

Top: *Photo courtesy of AquaFloat.*
Inset: *AquaFloat Flotation and Wellness Center is nestled in a downtown neighborhood populated with homes and medical offices.*

Dressing rooms are available to dry off and put yourself back together afterwards, but you can take the peaceful feelings with you when you go.

Massage, sauna, and hyperbaric oxygen therapy services are all on the menu in addition to the AquaFloat. Mix and match and find the best fit for your psyche.

Sensory deprivation treatment is what's achieved through floating, allowing floaters to achieve a meditative state without learning meditation.

CLANDESTINE COCKTAILS

What's the secret password?

There have been, no doubt, a number of secret speakeasies in Charlottesville's history, especially during the Prohibition era. Some will remember the short-lived Fellini's 9½, a hideaway tucked in a nook upstairs from the former Fellini's restaurant, which required a password to enter and enforced a dress code. Sadly, 9½ and Fellini's itself are but a memory, but other, better-hidden drinking holes have emerged to take their place.

Off the Downtown Mall, just up the hill a few steps from Violet Crown Theater, there's an unassuming alley on the left, just past Revolutionary Soup.

If you know, you know.

Be brave and walk right down that alley. See the unmarked wooden door with the carriage light hanging over it? Go ahead, open it.

SECRET WATERING HOLES

WHAT: Speakeasies and hidden establishments

WHERE: Lost Saint, 333 W. Main St.; Alley Light, 108 2nd St. S.W.

COST: Beverages start at $7

PRO TIP: Order the Dealer's Choice at the Alley Light, with a little guidance on preference of spirit or how sweet (or not) you'd like your cocktail. The mixologists on staff are at the top of their craft.

In the 1940s and '50s, Carroll's Tea Room was a popular establishment for university students. At the southwest corner of Emmett Street and Barracks Road, it was the most infamous watering hole of its day. Tea was not served! There was no Carroll!

Some secret bars are hard to find; follow the clues for a handcrafted cocktail. Inset: Photo courtesy of Hunter Chorey.

Inside, and up a flight of stairs, you'll find a completely unmarked treasure. The Alley Light's craft cocktails and French-inspired small plates menu are a special treat. If you know, you know. Ask the bartender for the dealer's choice.

On West Main Street, another speakeasy hides in plain view. Or does it? The Tavern and Grocery Restaurant is cover for the downstairs bar called Lost Saint. A cozy, converted-basement vibe, craft cocktails, and a late-night bar menu make Lost Saint a great place for a date or a gathering of conspiring friends.

TIME-TRAVEL TO A SODA FOUNTAIN

Where can you order a Mr. Coleman and a slice of pie?

There are two drugstores on the Downtown Mall. One is a national chain. The other is a locally owned vehicle for time travel. Timberlake's Drug Store delivers prescriptions free of charge within city limits. You can still find a bottle of Jean Naté body spray on its shelves. Once you've spent time browsing the glass cases and stocked shelves, you suddenly realize there's more to Timberlake's.

Beyond the retail front of the operation there's an old-timey lunch counter, its menu the same, one imagines, as it's been for the past 80 years. That, of course, is what makes it so good—the BLTs, the egg salad sandwiches, and the slices of pie served a la mode if you'd like. But don't forget to save room for a milkshake.

FAMILY-OWNED PHARMACY AND SODA FOUNTAIN

WHAT: Timberlake's Drug Store

WHERE: 322 E. Main St.

COST: Menu items start at about $4.

PRO TIP: The drug store is a full-service pharmacy that offers free delivery of prescriptions locally.

Order one of the men on the menu. Sandwiches, that is, all with masculine names like Mr. George (ham salad), Mr. Darden (egg salad with bacon), or Mr. Coleman (pastrami and Swiss on rye.)

Part nostalgic trip, part museum piece, photographs of regulars line the walls and invite browsing. They're not relics of the past—they're photos of the people who might be enjoying a Timberlake's lunch right that very moment.

Timberlake's Drug Store and Soda Fountain, the hidden restaurant with a lunch counter and soda fountain in the back.

Plop yourself down on a red vinyl stool at the counter, order up something you haven't had in a long, long time, and enjoy the memories that come flooding in, along with a surprising amount of sunlight.

Check the display window around the winter holidays to see a festive model train!

BOOK A TINY HOTEL

Are there places to stay right downtown?

Charlottesville has a thriving hotel industry. It seems like at least one new hotel opens every year. In addition, there are short-term rentals, bed-and-breakfast inns, and boutique hotels.

For an exceptionally interesting stay, try one of two super-tiny hotels right on the bustling Downtown Mall.

The first is The Townsman, which is so tiny it calls itself an "unhotel." We didn't even know that was a word! With four tiny rooms named after notable characters with a Charlottesville affiliation (Meriwether, Poe, Faulkner, and Secretariat), the boutique accommodations could not be more convenient. Skip on down the stairs to get your morning cup of joe at Mudhouse. Stumble home from a show at any one of five or six music venues on or near the mall. Shop and dine just a stone's throw from a place to store your packages, change outfits, or take a rest.

DOWNTOWN MALL ACCOMMODATIONS

WHAT: The Townsman and The Jeff Hotel

WHERE: 211 W. Main St. and 110 E. Main St., respectively

COST: Prices start at $118 for The Townsman and $149/night for The Jeff

PRO TIP: If you're looking for an exclusive concert experience, you can rent the top of the house at the Jefferson Theater, reserving the upper balcony with its own bartender and food service from one of two local restaurants. Ideal for 15 to 30 of your very best friends.

The Jefferson Theater is the oldest performance venue on the Downtown Mall; Harry Houdini once performed there.

Top: *A room at The Jeff. Photo courtesy of the Jeff Hotel.* Inset: *The Townsman "unhotel" exterior.*

Going to a show or two at the Jefferson Theater? Stay nearby (literally, a walk up the stairs next to the venue) for ultimate convenience and a quirky hotel experience at The Jeff Hotel. If you're looking for the privacy and convenience of a self-serve hotel, great views of the Downtown Mall, and a swanky, luxurious suite, The Jeff might be for you. If you're worried about noise from the Jefferson Theater below, put those thoughts aside. The hotel part of the building is soundproofed.

Choose from eight rooms, some tiny bed and bath nooks and others full suites with seating areas, giant flat-screen TVs, and large windows facing the Downtown Mall.

GET YOUR HANDS DIRTY

Ever have a strong urge to throw a pot?

Working with clay can be relaxing, frustrating, and, finally, gratifying. Trying to create clay artworks or functional pieces at home is nearly impossible. Enter City Clay, an awesome resource for the dirt-minded. A downtown studio offers equipment, creative space, classes, and more. Get to know a community of people who also enjoy sporting clay-spattered clothing.

Clay, in a number of varieties, is available for purchase. Wheels are available to reserve on site, or to rent to take home by the week.

Finished projects made with clay provided by City Clay can be fired in the on-site kilns and stored for artisans to pick up.

A gallery of products made by local artisans provides an on-site gift shop and inspiration for other makers in the space. Perhaps one day you will make something that will be displayed there, too.

DO-IT-YOURSELF POTTERY

WHAT: City Clay Pottery Studio

WHERE: 700 Harris St., #104

COST: $10/hour or $80/month

PRO TIP: If you want to find a one-of-a-kind gift or piece to add to your own collections, shop local artisans on the City Clay website or in the studio, where many excellent works are available for sale.

The Silk Mills Building is listed in the National Register of Historic Places collection for its architecture and history as the oldest surviving factory building in Charlottesville.

City Clay studio is inside the historic Silk Building in the city of Charlottesville.

If you're new to clay and uncertain, sign up for classes offered both on-site and virtually. Instructional videos are also available.

It's $10/hour for a drop-in session. Those who have basic pottery skills can obtain a membership at $80/month, entitling them to weekday studio access, a shelf for storage, and use of the pottery wheels.

City Clay is located in the Silk Building, a local historic structure, and has a super crafty vibe. Instructors have an array of styles and backgrounds, with impressive credentials and experience.

WITNESS A SPECTACLE

Will you support brawny gals for a good cause?

Charlottesville is the proud home of the first theatrical, philanthropic ladies arm-wrestling league, CLAW, the Charlottesville Lady Arm Wrestlers. We love our lady arm wrestlers! The names are as entertaining as the events (and the costumes). See The Homewrecker, Malice in Wonderland, Pushy Galore, Stiletto Southpaw, and Tropical Depression at their best! CLAW is a collection of local gals of various occupations, competing for bragging rights and upper body strength mojo, all while raising money for charitable organizations in town. Part carnival sideshow, part theatrical spectacle, and part sporting event, our town's baddest ladies dress up and throw down for charity.

Spectators are very much into the act. CLAWbucks, sold for cash, can be used to sway refs and judges, so competitors are encouraged to invite lots of friends with money.

CHARITY COMPETITIONS

WHAT: Charlottesville Ladies Arm Wrestling

WHERE: Champion Tap Room, 324 6th St. S.E.

COST: Ringside tickets $50

PRO TIP: Want to be a CLAW beneficiary? If you are a woman-founded or co-founded cause or project, (the minimum entry threshold), contact CLAW via clawville.org to find out more.

Ladies arm wrestling is not unique to Charlottesville. There are leagues in Chicago, Los Angeles, New Orleans, Washington, DC, and even a Southern Ladies Arm Wrestling League!

CLAW wrestlers and their entourages, fully decked out for feats of strength. Photos by Rich Tarbell.

The bouts typically take place at Champion Brewing Company's Tap Room tent, with premium tickets available at ringside. Proceeds go to a number of local ventures and charities, ranging from teen pregnancy support to kids' music programs. Among the charities supported is SARA, the Sexual Assault Resource Agency, which seeks to eliminate sexual violence and its impact by providing education, advocacy, and support to men, women, and children. Their vision is a community free from sexual violence.

The events are good, rowdy fun for a good cause.

PRIVATE COLLECTION GOES PUBLIC

Where can you hone your pinball skills?

Ophthalmologist and entrepreneur Dr. Paul Yates collects vintage pinball machines—no matter their condition. Dr. Yates takes the time to restore art, repair broken machines, and replace missing parts. As his collection grew, pinball machines filled his garage to overflowing. When the doctor could no longer store the games at home, he decided to share his collection with the public.

Dr. Yates opened Paul's Pinball Palace, allowing access to his museum of games to the public. Interest in the pinball emporium was enthusiastic. With an all-you-can-play $10 fee, it was a great form of evening entertainment.

As the business (and Dr. Yates) continued to collect machines, from pinball machines and video games to larger formats, including air hockey and the video game series Dance Dance Revolution, the arcade grew and grew. A small but dedicated group of fellow gamers donated

PINBALL PALACE

WHAT: Decades Arcade

WHERE: 221 Carlton Rd.

COST: $10

PRO TIP: Score a free entry with your arcade knowledge. Check Decades' social media presence every Thursday to play "Guess that Game." The first person to guess the game associated with the arcade art wins!

The oldest game in Dr. Yates's collection is a rare "woodrail" pinball machine from 1957. The game, Silver, has a wooden frame and lights behind the glass that indicate the player's score.

Decades Arcade, where a collection of pinball machines, Super Pac Man video game, and a vintage pinball game, Silver, are on display. Photos by Lindsay Daniels.

machines and their expertise for upkeep of the collection. Larger space opened in a warehouse in Belmont, and in the fall of 2018 Paul's Pinball Palace became Decades Arcade, so named because the games in the collection span the decades from the '50s to present day. Charlottesville's own Champion Brewing Company's warehouse is in the same building, so guests with a valid I.D. can sip a cold one while chasing that high score.

During the workweek, Decades hosts a local pinball league, has a dedicated game repair day, and hosts private events. Public hours are held on the weekends. Lucky for C'ville parents, the arcade has been flexible enough to open additional hours when kids are out of school, such as on spring break, snow days, or other unexpected gifts of leisure time. The fee remains a low $10 per gamer for an entire day's worth of play time.

WHEN ELIZABETH TAYLOR CAME TO TOWN

Is Charlottesville the next Hollywood?

Several films have used Charlottesville as a backdrop. Among them is *Evan Almighty*, the Steve Carell comedy that at one time filmed at an enormous ark in Crozet where the Old Trail neighborhood now resides.

Back in 1955, though, some iconic Hollywood stars arrived to film scenes for the classic movie *Giant*, which was shot in the Keswick area of Albemarle County. The cast and crew stuck around for a little while, staying at the Thomas Jefferson Inn. The Inn is now the Federal Executive Institute, which you can glimpse as you make your way along Emmet Street, about a mile from the university. The Institute is a training center for senior managers in the public sector and for governmental leaders, so unless you're one of those, you likely won't get to see the 14-acre property.

Another Hollywood connection should come to mind if you have occasion to travel John Warner Parkway, the connector between the city and Albemarle County. John Warner was a Republican senator in Virginia from 1979 to 2009, and the sixth husband of Elizabeth Taylor.

Rock Hudson, Elizabeth Taylor, and other cast members of the movie Giant *having dinner in Charlottesville, as captured by photographer Ed Roseberry. Photo courtesy of Charlottesville Albemarle Historical Society.*

But know that, once upon a time, Elizabeth Taylor, James Dean, and Rock Hudson all dined there. Fans of James Dean know that *Giant* was his last film.

When Hollywood comes to Charlottesville, locals like to get involved. Many of them are cast as extras in the films, as was true of both *Giant* and *Evan Almighty*.

HOLLYWOOD IN CHARLOTTESVILLE

WHAT: The filming of the movie *Giant*

WHERE: Federal Executive Institute, 1301 Emmet St. N.; Special Collections Library, 170 McCormick Rd.

COST: N/A

PRO TIP: The Holsinger Studio Collection at the Albert and Shirley Small Special Collections Library at the University of Virginia includes photographs of the *Giant* cast, taken by famed photographer Rufus W. Holsinger.

CHOOSE YOUR OWN PATH

Where is there an emerging state park?

South of the city of Charlottesville, within the boundaries created by State Route 20, Old Lynchburg Road, and Highway 64, fans of the outdoors will find Biscuit Run State Park. It's more of a park-in-progress at this point, but the land is there, and a handful of signs indicate its boundaries.

There are even a few trails in place, especially if you enter the park from the Route 20 end. Exciting plans are underway to develop the park with amenities common to other state parks in Virginia, including cabins to rent, a discovery visitors' center, equestrian accommodations, and trails for hikers and bikers. Parking will be available at a main entrance off Route 20.

The 1,200-acre park's main feature is a narrow but long waterway that runs the length of the property—that is the "Biscuit Run" for which the park is named. The property is lovely, forest and hills with pine, oak, and poplar for as far as the eye can see. To the north, Carter's Mountain, Monticello, and Montalto are visible.

Visitors may spot remains of old deer stands, ancient discarded car parts, and a couple of abandoned dwellings from long ago.

PARK IN PROGRESS

WHAT: Biscuit Run State Park

WHERE: Latitude 37°59'54" N., 78°31'03" W., / longitude 37.998327° N., 78.517399° W.

COST: Free

PRO TIP: A private trail connecting Biscuit Run Park to 5th St. Station runs between subdivisions between 5th St. Extended/Old Lynchburg Rd. and Avon St. Extended, so one access point is from the Wegman's parking lot at 5th St. Station.

As visitors come to enjoy the park now and in its eventual, more complete state, it's important to know that the park may very well never have happened.

In 1971, a developer from northern Virginia, L. J. Breeden, bought the 1,300-acre property for $1 million. He had every intention of developing the acreage into residential neighborhoods, and even a school. The purchase included Southwood Trailer Park, a property that still exists. Breeden's plans included doubling the size of the trailer park, a plan that met with strong opposition by neighbors.

In 2005, the Breeden family put the land up for auction, with the exception of acreage they kept for personal use. It went for $46.2 million to the highest bidder, a group of investors calling themselves Forest Lodge, LLC. The group intended to create a 5,000-home massive neighborhood, deforesting much of the property. The housing bubble burst in 2007, followed in short order by the recession. The group, unable to get approval for its development plans, rapidly lost money on the deal. To avoid further financial hardship, the group decided to donate the land to the state.

Their loss is our gain, as the area will be preserved and enjoyed by Albemarle families and visitors to the area for generations to come.

Take a hilly hike through forested Biscuit Run, the undeveloped state park.

Biscuit Run Studios remains on the original land and is the residence of the Breeden family. David Breeden founded the artists' space and for four decades created art on the premises, some of which can be seen on the Biscuit Run property today.

THE STEEPLE WITH NO PEOPLE

Who will say a prayer for the chapel?

At the east end of Market Street sits a perfectly picturesque church that features a 50-foot octagonal bell tower with green shutters. Its placement where the road comes to a V with Riverside Avenue makes it look less like a structure that was built on-site and more like the model of a chapel from your granddad's train set that grew overnight to life-size.

If that's how the chapel came to be, then it did so in 1887.

The building is historic, and so is the board of trustees formed to manage it. The trustees, however, are all ghosts at this point, long-deceased with no one to formally take their place.

The neighbors keep the place up, but it will continue to need serious work and an investment if it's going to last for another generation. The 1950s were the chapel's heyday, when it was used as gathering space for residents of all denominations to hold choir rehearsals, Sunday school, and Bible studies. The Woolen Mills neighborhood was a kind of company town, with many residents

HISTORIC CHAPEL

WHAT: Woolen Mills Chapel

WHERE: 1819 E. Market St.

COST: Free

PRO TIP: Scoot around the corner and up a slight hill to Woolen Mills itself and enjoy a meal or a beverage at Selvedge Brewing.

A historic industrial site, Woolen Mills was home to a working mill from the 1790s to the 1960s, and was, in part, property originally owned by Thomas Jefferson.

The Chapel at Woolen Mills and the refurbished Woolen Mills Factory, the location of Selvedge Brewing.

working at the manufacturing mill that was founded in the 1840s, churning out cloth for uniforms. The chapel provided gathering space away from work, in the heart of the community.

It's a beautiful sight, so unexpected when you happen upon it, and worth a drive, walk, or bike past.

TAKE A DIP

What's the best way to cool off on hot Virginia day?

Secret swimming holes are good because they're secret!
Commonly known spots like Blue Hole become real hot spots
on peak summer days. Befriend a local to gain access to the
most secluded spots for seasonal swims.

One we'll whisper to you about is called Guardrail Pool, a
not-so-secret yet mostly undiscovered spot just before you
reach the Ragged Mountain Reservoir.

HOW TO KEEP COOL

WHAT: Swimming holes

WHERE: 6796 Sugar Hollow is
the parking access to Blue Hole
and Snake Hole

COST: Free

PRO TIP: Wear a good pair of
water shoes. Swimming hole
rocks are slippery!

Riprap Hollow is a hike in
the Shenandoah National Park
that leads to a waterfall and
a freezing-cold, spring-fed
swimming hole.

Snake Hole is about as
unappealing a name for a
swimming hole as there is, but
it's a less-popular spot (the
name, perchance?) on the way
to Blue Hole. Snake Hole has
the benefit of being an easier
and shorter hike.

There's a semi-secret beach
in Darden Towe park on the Rivanna River, and several spots
with water access along the Rivanna Trail that allow you to
wade, dip your toes, or even go for a full-on swim. It's worth
being prepared for a dip any time you go for a hike during
Virginia's hot, humid summers, just in case you happen upon
an as-yet-undiscovered secret swimming hole.

Some favorite ways locals stay cool in the summer. Top: *Guardrail Pool. Photo by Dan Epstein.* Inset: *Paul's Creek Trail. Photo courtesy of Karen Klick.*

Paul's Creek Trail is a bit out of town in Nellysford. The swimming hole at the end of the trail offers natural rock formations that make for exciting water slides! It's a moderate mile or so hike to the falls and swimming spot.

RAILWAY LANDMARK

Why does an abandoned coal tower remain part of the city's landscape?

An urban stretch of million-dollar townhouses borders the train tracks that lead into downtown. Among them, as in cities all over the country, remains the original coal tower, which ceased to be used for loading coal onto trains over 30 years ago.

Why is there an unused, abandoned coal tower among properties owned by wealthy residents?

The coal tower's sometimes dark, sometimes arty history gives the area character. Charlottesville's first coal train arrived in 1850, and the legacy of the Chesapeake & Ohio line remains. (One of the city's most lauded restaurants, The C & O, is named for the railroad line and is located in a historic building.) Charlottesville certainly wouldn't be the city it is today if it weren't for its link to transportation and the coal industry.

The coal tower closed up shop in 1986.

In 1996, Live Arts Theater staged a production on the site. A play that opens and ends at a train station, *The Visit*, was the only official arts event held on the site.

The coal tower also has been the scene of both a double homicide and a suicide; both tragic incidents occurred in the early 2000s. The more recent development of new, surrounding, enormous single-family homes has reduced the likelihood of crime at the scene, a once-deserted property now

CITY LANDSCAPE

WHAT: Downtown coal tower

WHERE: E. Water St.

COST: Free

PRO TIP: The paved trail that links Carlton/Meade Aves. to Water St., past the coal tower and along the train tracks into downtown, is a nice, nearly flat place for a stroll or a jog.

Left: *Coal tower among the homes of C & O Row.* Inset: *It is one of only seven coal towers remaining in the country.*

populated by people driving by, walking dogs, and returning to their homes after a day at work.

A now-iconic part of the Charlottesville landscape, it has been depicted in paintings and is an instantly recognizable piece of the city's history.

A proposal to turn the area underneath and around the coal tower into a pocket park with a covered patio, bocce court, and dog park was approved by the Charlottesville Board of Architectural Review on August 21, 2018, but construction on that project has yet to begin.

A RIVER RUNS THROUGH IT

What waterway runs right through the city?

The Rivanna River winds its way through the city of Charlottesville and is easily accessible at various points if you have your own equipment and some floating/kayaking/canoeing know-how. If you're in town for just the day or lack boats and personal flotation devices (a legal requirement for river floating), we have the perfect solution for you. Just behind The Pie Chest on High Street, visitors will find Rivanna River Company.

This is the place to make your urban river trip easy and pleasant. Open from Memorial Day until Labor Day, Rivanna River Company offers guided trips and gear for self-guided adventures. This stretch of the Rivanna offers Class I and II rapids, so some trips are for the more experienced/adventurous.

All trips must be reserved online in advance, and prices start at $25 per guest.

In Charlottesville for the summer with kids? Consider Rivanna River Company's Watershed Adventure summer camps, with a variety of options for kids from six to 18 years of age.

If you're looking for a super-fun and original company outing, the shared memories created by a tubing or kayaking group trip can be just the thing.

The Rivanna takes its name from River Anne, named in honor of Queen Anne (1665–1714), who was the monarch of England and the Virginia Colony from 1702 until her death.

Top: *Photo courtesy of Melissa Garth Suttle. Rivanna River Outfitters offer canoe and kayak rentals in a convenient city location near the Rivanna River.*

As visitors drive through Charlottesville, it's easy to miss the fact that, on any busy summer work day, someone is likely floating down the river, fishing, or just taking it easy.

In the market for some paddling gear of your own? Keep an eye out for the company's end-of-season sale, in which they offer used equipment for a song.

RIVER RENTALS AND GUIDES

WHAT: Rivanna River Company

WHERE: 1518 E. High St.

COST: $25 per guest

PRO TIP: Get a season pass ranging from $195 to $595, allowing for quick and easy rentals all summer long.

OBSCURE EATERY

Is that a restaurant in a parking garage?

With dishes like crab casserole and duck, Tastings may be the finest restaurant ever found in a parking garage. With so many restaurants in more obvious venues, it would not be surprising at all if you were to overlook the modest exterior.

Bill Curtis is a man the *New York Times* once called a leading authority on Virginia wines. He is certainly that, as well as the proprietor and chef at Tastings. The venue calls itself a fully integrated wine shop and restaurant, and at first glance you may think you've wandered into just a wine shop. But the food, heavy on the seafood and luxe appetizers, is nothing short of fancy. Chef William's Crabmeat Casserole is a menu staple.

Tastings is the place to take your out-of-town parents, to have a private lunch date, or to enjoy a special wine-tasting occasion. With an extraordinarily large menu of wines by the glass, you can take the opportunity to explore varietals unavailable in other area restaurants and bars.

HIDDEN RESTAURANT

WHAT: Tastings of Charlottesville

WHERE: 502 E. Market St.

COST: Entrees start at $12

PRO TIP: If seafood is the key to your heart, Tastings is the best restaurant in town.

Court Square Tavern, a pub in the basement of the 500 Court Square building, is a sister restaurant to Tastings.

Top: *Tastings, the restaurant.* Inset: *Bill Curtis, owner of Tastings.*

Sign up for Bill's weekly newsletters to be in the know about the most current bottles of wine available and to receive Bill's recommendations for various occasions. There are also updates to the menu so readers know when to get in on lobster, veal, or elk. Tastings truly has one of the most eclectic and gourmet menus in town.

For the full experience, make a reservation and ask for wine pairings with each course. Bill will be happy to oblige.

THE HOUSE THAT BARRINGER BUILT

What's the story behind that gorgeous Queen Anne mansion?

One of the loveliest historic properties in the Charlottesville area has to be Barringer Mansion. Built in 1895, it was once the home of Dr. Paul Barringer, UVa professor, scientist, physician, and one-time chairman of faculty at the University of Virginia.

The grand Queen Anne-style house is notable for its tower, columns, and many chimneys. Architectural enthusiasts will enjoy seeing the mansion's elaborate turret with garland frieze and three styles of windows.

Barringer is credited with playing a major role in developing the University's hospital. However, recent discussions have centered on the fact that Barringer was a white supremacist, as shown in an essay he shared in 1900, in which he insisted that African Americans benefited from slavery. As a result, UVa is taking steps to remove Barringer's name from the historic property and other places around Grounds.

Barringer went on from UVa to be the sixth president of Virginia Tech.

La Maison Française, Barringer House at the University of Virginia, is the immersive, French-language residence for students.

The university bought the mansion, which once upon a time hosted Theodore Roosevelt and William Jennings Bryan, in 1985, and it is now home to UVa's center for French culture. Converted to apartments in 1967, the building is ideal for la Maison Française, where all resident students commit to speaking French in the common areas of the house.

WINE THROUGH TIME

How did the business of wine become so big in Charlottesville?

In 1870, William Hotopp kicked off the events that led to Charlottesville becoming a renowned town for wine lovers when he planted grapevines with the purpose of establishing a winery. His wines were popular: what the Albemarle Charlottesville Historical Society called "pure and healthful, low-alcohol table wines of medium grade."

In 1873, a handful of other German immigrants pooled their resources to found the Monticello Wine Company, earning awards at the 1876 Vienna Exposition and the 1878 Paris World's Fair for their "Extra Virginia Claret," thus putting Monticello Wine Company and Charlottesville on the oenophiles' map. By 1890, Monticello Wine Company was the largest winery in the South, with a 200,000-gallon production capacity.

Prohibition killed the business for a time, and the winery's original building burned down in 1937, but the wine manager's home stands today, on Wine Street, of course.

Wine and wineries are big business in Central Virginia. There are 35 within a 30-mile radius of the city. Monticello Wine Company, the original brand, has been revitalized in recent years by the Smith family, owners of Afton Mountain Vineyards.

THE HOUSE THAT WINE BUILT

WHAT: Monticello Wine Company at Wine Street

WHERE: 212 Wine St.

COST: A bottle of today's Monticello Wine Company wine will run you $21 and up.

PRO TIP: Plan your visit around the Monticello Wine Trail and plan to taste as many vintages as the area has to offer.

Monticello Wine Company's mark on Charlottesville can still be seen in its growing wine industry and on Wine Street in the city.

The Hotopp family were prominent Charlottesville residents. Their estate was what is now Pen Park, where research has been undertaken recently to learn the history of unmarked graves of enslaved people on the site.

WHITE DEER SIGHTINGS

Was that a ghost, or a unicorn?

From time to time, Charlottesville residents manage to capture images of white deer strolling through yards or leaping into forested land that borders neighborhoods. Is a white deer a mythical Patronus? Or an animal spirit wandering among us?

They are real, as anyone who has gotten a closeup look will tell you. But what are they?

White deer can be either albino, leucistic, or piebald. Albinism in deer is the rarest of the three, and is detected animals with pink eyes, blindness, and a total absence of pigmentation. Leucistic deer are often blotchy or have uneven pigmentation. It may be tough to tell the difference as a white or perhaps only mostly white deer dashes across your field of vision. A piebald deer is generally a mixed brown and white deer.

What we appear to have in Charlottesville stems from a genetic mutation passed down through generations, so most

GHOST OR UNICORN?

WHAT: Albino deer

WHERE: Reports of white deer sightings come from the neighborhoods of Fry's Spring and Johnson Village: some have been spotted along the John W. Warner Parkway and near the South Fork Rivanna River Reservoir; another was seen along the west side of 5th St., between Cleveland and Bailey.

COST: Free

NOTABLE: A large population of white, leucistic deer exists in Seneca, NY, as a result of a large, fenced area around a 10,000-acre closed munitions plant that is a holdover from the Cold War. The barrier has caused inbreeding among the deer, creating generations of the white deer.

Native Americans attribute the sign of prophecy to come with the vision of a white deer.

An albino doe in a Charlottesville backyard. Photos by Peyton Williams.

likely, what locals report and capture are all from the same line of white, albino deer.

The feeling of having witnessed a rare, mystical being is not without its truth, as the genetic mutations that accompany albinism lead to a more difficult existence for the deer and trouble surviving in the wild.

If you are gifted with a glimpse, count yourself among the lucky, and wish a deer family well.

GET A CONFIDENCE BOOSTER

Want to learn to fly?

Part dance studio, part aerial arts training course, Phoenix Dance Studio has been empowering people, especially women, to find their strength for more than 15 years. It is the place in Charlottesville where a person can go to learn to pole dance or to learn an exotic dance routine in a safe and supportive space.

The studio is a sanctuary, with experienced instructors dedicated to promoting physical, mental, and emotional fitness.

In addition to the sexy stuff, Phoenix is the only place in town where a person can go to learn the aerial arts. Ever dreamed of flying through the air on a trapeze? Perhaps you've admired the work of performers climbing to the ceiling using only long strands of silk fabric?

Phoenix mixes art with strength training for all students.

The aerial arts programs are for students of all ages and genders. There are even kids' classes teaching performance skills with the lyra, an aerial hoop you may have seen under a big top tent once upon a time.

Phoenix prides itself on providing a supportive environment for learners at all times. For some, especially for exotic dance, a private or semi-private lesson might be preferred, and is available.

DANCE LESSONS FOR GROWNUPS

WHAT: Phoenix Dance Studio

WHERE: 629 Berkmar Cir.

COST: $20 per class, $55 for a private lesson, and $30 per person for a two- or three-person, semi-private class. Advance registration required.

PRO TIP: The Femme Fatales, a group of the dance studio's advanced students, is available to perform for exhibitions and special events.

Aerial arts, exotic dance, and kids' classes.
Photos courtesy of Phoenix Dance Studio.

As a special treat, the Phoenix Dance Studio ladies put on a public performance once a year or so. Keep an eye out for special burlesque and aerial performances around town, and, if you're inspired, call 434-293-1127 to find out more about lessons for yourself.

Strip Down, Rise Up (2021) is a Netflix documentary exploring the world of pole dancing outside of strip clubs.

ACKNOWLEDGING HISTORY (page 48)

MICHOACÁN SPECIALTIES (page 42)

Photo courtesy of Jody Saunders

SNUGGLE A BABY GOAT (page 142)

GET IN SOME STEPS (page 162)

A CONGREGATION WITH HISTORY (page 24)

HORSING AROUND (page 170)

WITNESS A SPECTACLE (page 62)

THE EXTRAS AT MONTPELIER (page 186)

ART TO EXPERIENCE (page 156)

A SECRET ROSE GARDEN (page 20)

MURALS ALL OVER TOWN (page 174)

THE "IN" CROWD (page 4)

HAVE A FEAST!

Where can you find an impressive cheese counter?

A longtime Charlottesville resident introduced us to Feast! when we first moved to town. Hidden within a complex that has a couple of storefront restaurants and a bakery facing the street, it's not so easy to find. A casual visitor might miss it completely.

Feast! is part gourmet grocery, part lunch spot, part gift shop. The lunch options are delicious, and it's our favorite stop for a fancy picnic basket fill-up.

What people swoon over, though, is the cheese counter. Whether you want to try a taste before you buy or you're seeking advice to build your own charcuterie tray, the Feast! cheesemonger is there for you. They also put together beautiful cheese boards for any size event. The selection is top-notch and there are plenty of items in the store to complement your purchase.

INCREDIBLE CHEESE SELECTION

WHAT: Feast!

WHERE: 416 W. Main St.

COST: Varies

PRO TIP: In the same building, find Albemarle Baking Company, a perfect place to complement your selections from Feast! with some outstanding baked goods.

In 2009, Feast's owners started the nonprofit Local Food Hub to assist local farmers who needed more time for cultivation rather than distribution. In 2019, Local Food Hub transferred distribution to 4PFoods, which delivers 7,500 pounds of food per month to underserved communities across DC, Maryland, and Virginia.

Top: *Cheeseboard from Feast!*
Photos courtesy of Feast!

If you're not much of a cook and yet have somehow promised to wow someone with a homemade meal, a stop at Feast! may be just the thing to bail you out. Head to the refrigerated case in the back left corner and select some fancy ravioli and a complementary sauce. Grab a bottle of wine and a baguette. Dinner is saved!

Local items abound, so Feast! is the perfect place to swing by and pick up a gift. And you might as well time it with lunch, so you can pick up a turkey, brie, and cranberry panini; the tofu bahn mi; the chicken, cheddar, and fig sandwich; or one of the excellent gourmet salads! Before you check out, make sure you add to your collection a little treat, like some salted caramels or fancy cookies. You deserve it!

SECRET SLEDDING HILLS

Where to go in the snow?

It's admittedly rare, but it does happen. Snow in Charlottesville! The snowiest season on record was 2009–10, when 56.8 inches of the stuff fell between December and March. When it happens, kids and adults alike head for the hills to make the most of a super snow day.

Skiers and snowboarders watch the forecast carefully. When conditions are right, it might be worth an hour's drive to the Wintergreen ski resort to get in a few runs while the snow holds out. Wintergreen also makes its own snow, but everyone knows the real stuff is much better.

If you're in town, and especially if you have young kids, load up the sleds and head to some of the best sledding available in this short-lived winter wonderland. Helmets are highly recommended, as trees and other sledders are frequent crash-traps.

Washington Park is the king of all the sledding hills, with its steep, grassy slope and enough room for large gangs of kids to zip safely downhill.

For short and steep runs, try the hillsides that drop from Gentry Lane near Walker Elementary School or the hill behind Burnley-Moran Elementary.

The Charlottesville High School property has lots of great hills and plenty of area to spread out, as well as the advantage of being a walkable distance for many neighborhoods.

SLEDDING SPOTS

WHAT: Booker T. Washington Park Sledding Hill

WHERE: 1001 Preston Ave.

COST: Free

PRO TIP: Caught by surprise with a pop-up snowstorm and no sled? The Downtown Mall CVS location often has a stash of sleds to sell.

Sometimes we get snow! Kids sled in parks and on hills around Charlottesville. Top and inset photos courtesy of Cindy Kirst; bottom photo courtesy of Kate Duvall.

Piedmont Virginia Community College has some great sledding space as well. The bonus for all these school sledding spots is the availability of lots of parking. Pack up your sleds and a thermos of hot chocolate, put on your snow pants, hats, and gloves, and prepare for an exhilarating ride!

The first of three storms in the 2009–10 season came on Friday, December 18. Two inches of snow fell between 4 and 5 p.m., bringing the evening commute and holiday traffic to a halt, with cars abandoned all along Interstate 64, US Route 29, and in neighborhoods.

CLIMB ABOARD A KEELBOAT

What was it like to travel with Lewis and Clark?

The Lewis and Clark Exploratory Center is tucked so far back in Darden Towe Park you practically have to lead an expedition to find it. Charlottesville sits on land originally occupied by the Monacan Nation, and the Lewis and Clark Exploratory Center exists where native American people used to live. Our written accounts come from the journals of Meriwether Lewis, who was born in Albemarle County, and William Clark. Clark's parents owned the land adjacent to Darden Towe Park. With roots in the area and curriculum based on their journals and travel notes, the center is named after both explorers.

EXPEDITION HISTORY

WHAT: Lewis and Clark Exploratory Center

WHERE: Darden Towe Park

COST: Event tickets start at $10/person

PRO TIP: Check out the organization's annual fundraiser, the Portable Feast, which occurs in the fall.

The Lewis and Clark expedition began with the Missouri River in the Midwest and ended with the Columbia River, which runs through Washington and Oregon.

The Exploratory Center, right on the banks of the Rivanna River, features a life-sized keelboat replica that's fun to see and imagine the explorers using on their journey along the Missouri River. It's fun for kids to climb on, too.

The facility is host to members of local indigenous groups sharing educational programming about their history in the area. Hands-on activities and exhibitions follow the path of the expedition virtually; visitors can explore its impact and the lessons that were learned along the way.

Visitors are invited to climb and explore a keelboat and other boat replicas at the Lewis and Clark Exploratory Center.

With a focus on using the expedition as a tool for learning about history, exploration, transportation, the arts, science, the natural environment, and native cultures, the center offers a variety of programs for children and adults. Art, mapmaking, 3D printing, and carpentry all come into play.

The facility also is available to rent for small events such as team building, corporate retreats, large family gatherings, and more. The center specializes in school field trips, but also encourages visitors and planned events of all kinds. Nearby trails along the banks make it an ideal setting for education, creative work, and deep thinking.

York, a Black man enslaved by William Clark, was crucial to the success of Lewis and Clark's expedition through hunting, discovering new plants and animals, caring for the ill, and communicating with the Native Americans. At the end of the expedition, Clark broke his promise and refused to free York.

OFF-SEASON FOOTBALL

What's a die-hard football fan supposed to do in the spring?

Pro football exhibition games don't start until late summer, and college and high school games don't get going until school is back in session in the fall. That gap between the Super Bowl in late January or early February and the early fall can seem like a lifetime!

Enter adult, semi-pro football, the answer to all your local football desires. The Virginia Silverbacks play right in town, on the field at Monticello High School, with a season that runs from March until May. The team is part of the United Eastern Atlantic Football League, and the players take their game on the road to compete against teams in Baltimore and Virginia Beach when not at home.

Players come from throughout the region and, as semi-pro players, are able to get paid for their performance on the field, although sadly not enough to make a full-time career out of it. Some players have day jobs and other are retired from working life, leaving them with plenty of time to stay in shape, practice, and play football.

SEMI PRO FOOTBALL

WHAT: Virginia Silverbacks

WHERE: 1400 Independence Way

COST: Games are $8/ticket

PRO TIP: Catch a team practice over the lunch hour at Buford Middle School.

Allen Lynch, a white-haired, 65-year-old, esteemed UVa professor of politics and expert in Russian foreign policy, is a placekicker for the Silverbacks.

Semi-pro football players on the Virginia Silverbacks team. Photos courtesy of the Virginia Silverbacks.

TINY CONCERT VENUE

What's the most unusual concert venue in town?

We guarantee this music venue will totally escape your notice when a concert is not under way. It is, after all, a tiny garage. However, this unassuming spot has attracted big crowds. During the spring and summer months, the Garage opens and fans flock to the grassy knoll in Emancipation Park, directly across from its doors.

Home to not only concerts but also art exhibits, dance parties, potlucks, and other creative gatherings, this public-yet-private venue can be reserved by community members by request.

In 2008, the owner of the space, Christ Episcopal Church, converted its single-car garage into a small public arts space. The garage, once the parking spot for the church's organist (who now presumably must find street parking like the rest of us) then became the Garage, capital G. The Garage's director set out with a goal of providing the area with quality music, visual art, and other communal activities for anyone who happened to stroll by. Within a year of its inception, the Garage was well-established as Charlottesville's most unique concert venue.

UNUSUAL CONCERT SPACE

WHAT: The Garage

WHERE: 100 E. Jefferson St.

COST: Free

PRO TIP: Get takeout from nearby tiny-window restaurant Luce for fresh, homemade pasta with delicious toppings, and enjoy dinner while you listen to the show.

Before rising to fame, The Lumineers once played the space.

The Garage is Charlottesville's tiny, perfect concert venue, with plentiful seating on the lawn in the park across the street. Photos courtesy of the Garage.

The Garage's founder, Sam Bush, said, "The vision for the Garage was to create a space that invited conversation and communal interaction. The smallness of the Garage allows groups of people to gather for an art opening, workshop, or potluck dinner and engage with each other in an especially intimate and personal way. The Garage has always walked a fine line between public and private—on the one hand, it's accessible to anyone who walks by; on the other hand, it allows people to feel like they are a part of something special."

The audience takes a seat on the lawn of the park across the street, and during performances cars travel the road between musicians and their fans.

THE REAL HIGHLAND

What happened to former President James Monroe's house?

Every year, half a million people flock to Monticello, the home of Thomas Jefferson. Right around the corner, though, is Highland, the Albemarle County home of James Monroe. From 1837 until recently, the property was called Ash Lawn-Highland, because Alexander Garrett, an owner down the line from Monroe, changed the name from Highland (what Monroe called it) to Ash Lawn. It was in 2016 that the executive director of the estate made the move to rechristen the home with its original name.

Much more has been uncovered about the estate in Monroe's time, and a tour gives history buffs all they desire, with rich background.

The original home in which Monroe lived burned down in a fire. Archeological discoveries as recent as a few years ago have rewritten the history shared at the historic site. Like many historic sites of this era, the legacy of enslaved people is part of the story. Highland tours address the generations of enslaved people who lived on the property and endeavor to share their stories, as well.

THE FIFTH PRESIDENT'S HOUSE

WHAT: Monroe's Highland

WHERE: 2050 James Monroe Pkwy.

COST: $10/visitor, $150/group for the Behind-the-Scenes tour

PRO TIP: Spring for the Behind-the-Scenes tour and get a look at the 1818 presidential guesthouse as it is re-curated.

While the University of Virginia owns many of the sites in town, Highland is an exception. The property belongs to the College of William & Mary, Monroe's alma mater.

Top: *Highland. Photo by K. Carpenter.* Inset: *Family-friendly, self-guided tour. Photo by Heather Balmat.* Bottom: *Rustic trail. Be sure to check into the visitors' center, even if you're just hiking the rustic trails.*

Several events make great use of the lawn at Highland, including the Albemarle County Fair, many outdoor concerts, and our personal favorite, the annual sheep shearing. There's nothing cuter than a freshly shorn sheep! The event also features wool-related educational presentations like carding and spinning, with demonstrations of fiber arts from Monroe's time.

Don't miss the rustic Highland Trails, a lovely, educational hike with options from easy to moderate to strenuous. They are the best-marked hiking trails in the area.

'HOOS HOUSE, OR CAMPBELL HOUSE ON LEWIS MOUNTAIN

Whose house is 'Hoos House?

Some call it the 'Hoos House. Others, with more knowledge, call it the Campbell House, so-called for the family that owns the house today. It is, geographically speaking, the house on Lewis Mountain. The house, designed in 1909 and built in 1912, does not, in fact, have any relationship to the University of Virginia, despite its proximity and the many rumors that have plagued its existence. The home is visible from the university Grounds and, from atop the mountain, has 360-degree views of much of Charlottesville and the university. Made of stone and surrounded by a 42-acre property, the house is quite grand, with 14-foot ceilings throughout and fireplaces in every room.

Built by Brigadier General John Watts Kearny, the home was for a time also known as Kearny's House. Because of its size and visibility from the university, visitors often mistakenly identify the Lewis Mountain property as Monticello, but nothing could be further from the truth. To date, no owner has attended or had any affiliation with the university.

University tour guides gone rogue like to share one particular myth about the house. It goes like this:

> *Every 'Hoo down in 'Hooville liked college a lot.*
> *But the Grinch,*
> *Who lived just above C'ville,*
> *Did not.*

If you're familiar with How the Grinch Stole Christmas, you've heard of the Whos, the residents of Dr. Seuss's Whoville. A widespread myth is that Dr. Seuss, a.k.a. Theodor Geisel, lived in the Lewis Mountain house and that the 'Hoos house refers to his book.

The mysterious mansion that can be seen from the Grounds of UVa, rumored to be the home of Dr. Seuss. Photo courtesy of The Holsinger Collection, Albert and Shirley Small Special Collections Library, University of Virginia.

Not so! Geisel was from Minnesota, not Albemarle County. The origin of "Hoo" in the context of University of Virginia students comes from "wahoo," which comes from, allegedly, the wahoo fish, known for being able to drink twice its weight. And that's the truth about the 'Hoos and the house on Lewis Mountain.

'HOOS HOUSE

WHAT: House on Lewis Mountain

WHERE: 1 Lewis Mtn. Pkwy.

COST: Not currently for sale or open to the public

PRO TIP: Celebrated local architect Eugene Bradbury designed the house on Lewis Mountain, in addition to several other notable homes in the area.

The Kearny family referred to their Virginia mountaintop estate as Onteora, after a mountain in the Catskills where they had previously had an estate.

UNTOASTED FAVORITE

Where can you get the best bagel?

There are cities famous for the quality of their bagels. Some are fond of bagels found in New York. Bah, we say. In Charlottesville, bagels are Bodo's and Bodo's alone. The legendary bagels are so cherished that people from out of town make sure they stock up and fill their freezer to satisfy their cravings until the next visit.

Bodo's started with one location on Emmet Street. Preston Avenue was the second location, and another was added at the Corner at the University of Virginia (a sign announcing "coming soon" was present for a full two years before the Corner location opened). All three low-cost, high-volume eateries churn out bagels, bagel sandwiches, salads, and sides like a well-oiled machine.

If you show up at any Bodo's location and the line is out the door, persist! Locals know of the efficiency of the operation. The line may be long, but the service is swift. You'll not find a smoother food operation in town.

A couple of pro tips: Know your order before you get to the counter or others around you will be filled with consternation and peg you as a tourist. And don't ask for your bagel to be toasted! Bodo's doesn't toast, and it's one of the reasons they're able to get you in and out the door fast. If you want to toast your bagels, get them to go, and prep them as you like in your own kitchen. They'll even slice up to three per order at no extra cost.

Here's a lesson on forming your order: choose from ten bagel flavors including plain, sesame, cinnamon raisin, whole wheat, or

Right: Bodo's egg salad on an everything bagel. Photo courtesy of Cyd Oldham. Inset: Bodo's Preston location.

everything. For a sandwich, consider eggs, sausage, deli meats, egg salad, and a variety of cheeses. Many additions are available to top it off, including avocado, hummus, olive spread, fig jam, lettuce, and tomato. If you're a bagel and cream cheese purist, there's that, too, with a selection of flavors. Take a tour around the menu until you settle on your favorite, and prepare to order it often.

Despite some of the locations having an inherited drive-thru window, before the COVID-19 pandemic that began in 2020, no Bodo's location had ever offered a drive-thru option.

TINY WINDOW, BIG FLAVORS

What big lunch can you get through a tiny takeout window?

Some of Charlottesville's best restaurants are so tiny and unassuming, you might miss out big-time if you're not paying attention. Vu Noodles is certainly one of these. A tiny brick building with a window for ordering and takeout and a handful of tiny two-tops or bistro tables in its outdoor patio are all there is to see. But the flavors produced within are huge!

The history of the space goes back just a little way. Locals will remember with great fondness the Flat Creperie, where chef Lauren McRaven cranked out sweet and savory traditional and modern takes on authentic French crepes. The tiny kitchen, tucked between the Jefferson Theater's back-door loading dock and Petite Marie Bette, still produces food with ethnic flavor, but this time it's Vietnamese.

Owner Julie Vu Whitaker began business as a home kitchen caterer, but demand

GREAT VIETNAMESE FOOD

WHAT: Vu Noodles

WHERE: 111 E. Water St.

COST: Entrées start at $10

PRO TIP: Opt to add chia seeds or tapioca pearls to your iced tea or coffee for a special treat.

Vu Noodles proprietor Julie Vu Whitaker was born in Vietnam and immigrated to Waynesboro, Virginia, at just eight years old. Julie learned to cook traditional Vietnamese dishes from her mother.

Vu Noodles, the tiny Water Street restaurant, is a lunchtime takeout favorite.

for the brand's offerings grew quickly. From its current Water Street venue, try Vu's excellent caramelized onion tofu noodle dish, the fantastic Bahn Mi sandwich, the Pho, or any of the delicious bowls. Wet your whistle with Vietnamese iced coffee or a mango iced tea.

Quick and friendly service, lots of vegetarian and vegan options, and a convenient stop for lunch while you visit downtown are all reasons to seek out the Vu Noodles window.

A WALK IN THE WOODS

Where is a bucolic garden hidden?

At the intersection of Reservoir Road and Foxhaven Farm is a 280-acre treasure well worth exploring. Foxhaven Farm, with its vast fields, wide trails, mountain climbs, and pine forests, is a gorgeous place to spend a day. Choose the trails that go up to Round Top, a ridge overlooking the Boar's Head property and Birdwood Golf Course, or stick to the flatter walkways around the fields for easier strolls.

Once the property of garden and hiking enthusiast Jane Heyward, most of the land is now owned by the University of Virginia Foundation. A beloved former resident's private property, including a home and several outbuildings, is found at the end of the Foxhaven Farm driveway.

Enter the property from Reservoir Road and park in the small lot to the left. Trails begin in the field to the left of the parking area. Or, continue down the side of Foxhaven Farm Road until you reach the Jane Heyward Gardens on the right. Review the map before you explore the gardens to avoid trespassing at the private residence there. A springtime visit reveals a carpet of Lenten roses and periwinkle. The whole garden is enchanting.

HIDDEN GARDENS

WHAT: Foxhaven Farm

WHERE: Reservoir Road and Foxhaven Farm, or access from Birdwood Golf Course/ Boar's Head Inn

COST: Free

PRO TIP: Pack a picnic, a blanket, or some camp chairs and enjoy a peaceful lunch in a beautiful setting in the field to the right of the parking lot as you enter the property.

Left: *The bucolic Jane Heyward Garden at Foxhaven Farm.* Right: *Rustic farm trails offer an easy hike, while trails up the mountain are more strenuous and rewarding.*

Enhance your enjoyment of Jane's garden by reading about the generous, vibrant, active woman who had great love for the land and of growing things and exploring the mountains—and who made it possible. Janeheyward.blogspot.com is a collection of remembrances of Jane by the people in the community who knew her best.

Jane Heyward also was responsible for the donation of the 755-acre Fortune's Cove in Nelson County, near Lovingston. This nature preserve is maintained by The Nature Conservancy.

URBAN TREASURE HUNT

Are you a fan of geocaching?

Geocaching is a high-tech scavenger hunt. It's no surprise that outdoors-loving Charlottesville would be warm to the idea of this outside activity.

Participants follow clues and GPS coordinates to find "treasure" to log or document. Geocaching apps are used to check off a series of stops.

Enthusiasts in the area have created many themed geocaching maps. Find the treasure hunt that interests you most, or use the app to investigate any area you might visit. There are geocache games with history clues, university stops, downtown/city locations, and more.

The final cache is the big payoff: a container where players find a logbook and sometimes a treasure. Log your find and follow the directions to the next game, or see if the creator wants you to leave something behind.

Finally, an activity kids and parents can agree upon! An outdoor activity that provides some exercise, some logistical and cognitive skill-building, and the opportunity to do something together, geocaching makes for a great family outing.

TREASURE HUNTING

WHAT: Geocaching

WHERE: Follow the coordinates.

COST: Free

PRO TIP: Peruse the app to learn about the game before you set out on a treasure hunt.

There are more than 457 geocaches around Charlottesville!

Geocaching is popular with outdoor-loving, active Charlottesville residents. Photos courtesy of Holly Duke, Aimee Carter, and Pat Belisle.

GEORGIA O'KEEFFE SLEPT HERE

What famous painter got her jumpstart at UVa?

In 2018, The Fralin Museum of Art at the University of Virginia held a special exhibition featuring the artwork of Georgia O'Keeffe and her time at UVa. For many, this was the first they learned of the famed artist's years at the university or had seen her drawings, many of them sketches and paintings of familiar sights around the university Grounds.

O'Keeffe, born in Wisconsin, only came to Charlottesville as an adult when her mother and sisters moved to the area and rented a house in the city in 1909. O'Keeffe first took a summer course for art teachers at the university in 1912, then returned to teach art at the university over the summers of 1913 through 1916.

The initial visit to Charlottesville came after O'Keeffe's father's bankruptcy and her parents' separation. Those events contributed to O'Keeffe's four-year dry spell in painting and a loss of confidence

WHERE GEORGIA O'KEEFFE RETURNED TO PAINTING

WHAT: Georgia O'Keeffe's mother's house

WHERE: 1212 Wertland St.

COST: Free

PRO TIP: The Fralin has maps of a Georgia O'Keeffe walking tour around Grounds. The map includes images of her work from her time in Charlottesville. The map is free to any museum visitor. Museum admission also is free.

O'Keeffe is known for her paintings of flowers, so it's surprising to most that, among her more than 2,000 paintings, only 200 are of flowers.

The house where a painter frozen with artist's block got her mojo back and went on to become famous.

and creativity. She credited her time at the university with helping her return to her craft; the city and the school grounds helped to restart her creative inspiration and desire to paint.

During her time in Charlottesville, the artist produced some lovely renderings of the Rotunda, as well as many other works that display her progress and growth as a painter.

The home in which she lived with her family sits at 1212 Wertland. A historical marker stands near the property at the corner of Wertland and 12 ½ streets.

IS THAT TONY HAWK?

What park got a famous boost from a pro?

It's a little-known fact that Charlottesville has one of the finest skate parks anywhere in the region. Carefully planned, designed, and built with input from avid skaters and dedicated designers, the park is top-notch, covering two acres of McIntire Park. The recreation division of the city set out to create something that would be a destination attraction for Charlottesville, as well as a welcome addition to the recreational offerings for local people. The plans for the park were so well thought out, that an application to famed skateboarder Tony Hawk's foundation granted the park $25,000 in funding during the building process. Now, that's an endorsement!

Kids and adults alike enjoy the park at their own risk. It features beginners' areas and more pro-level jumps and bowls.

BEST PLACE TO PRACTICE YOUR OLLIE

WHAT: Charlottesville Skate Park

WHERE: McIntire Park

COST: Free

PRO TIP: On social media, Tony Hawk has made quite a joke out of the fact that while he's actually a celebrity, no one seems to recognize him when he's out and about. If you spot him at Charlottesville's skatepark, or really anywhere, it might earn you free skateboarding gear.

Tony Hawk is a professional skateboarder who made his $140-million fortune through his skateboard company, Birdhouse, and through licensed video games.

Charlottesville Skate Park is in the city limits near the Brooks Family YMCA. The park is for skaters of all levels of ability.

Thoughtful siting put the skate park near parking and its own restroom. The completed park is popular and draws crowds of skaters of all skill levels on good weather days.

Once you're done skating, or if you're just providing transportation to the skate park for younger kids, don't miss the walking trails and the emerging Botanical Park of the Piedmont, as it develops on the grounds nearby. The Dogwood Vietnam Memorial shares space in the park as well, and is notable as the first civic/public memorial in the United States dedicated to those who gave their lives and served in Vietnam. It's a monument about which Charlottesville can be proud.

HOOPS WITH A MESSAGE

Where can you catch an inspiring basketball game?

In 1980, six local athletes formed a basketball league like no other in the region. The Charlottesville Cardinals wheelchair basketball team was created to provide athletes with disabilities an opportunity for exercise and competitive recreation. The Cardinals also educate the public about the capabilities of people with disabilities. Since its formation, more than 700 area athletes with disabilities have participated with the team.

The team's lineup includes players of all genders and a wide range of ages. The youngest current player is 25 and the oldest is 66. The Charlottesville Cardinals compete in the National Wheelchair Basketball Association and also perform numerous demonstrations at schools, churches, and community events.

The team of athletes also has assisted numerous community groups to raise funds for various causes.

The Cardinals perform across the US, Canada, and Puerto Rico. Locals can sometimes catch them as the halftime entertainment at University of Virginia basketball games. Check the schedule on the team's website and take in a game at Key Rec Center.

BASKETBALL THAT EDUCATES AND INSPIRES

WHAT: Cardinals Wheelchair Basketball

WHERE: 815 Cherry Ave.

COST: Free, but donations are gratefully accepted

PRO TIP: In 2018–19 the Cardinals posted their 17th straight 20+ win season, finishing the year ranked 16th in the nation.

Cardinals Wheelchair Basketball players show off their skills at Key Rec Center. Photos courtesy of Cardinals Wheelchair Basketball.

Nearby Harrisonburg, Virginia, Parks & Rec holds an annual Shamrock 5K Trail Run, with proceeds benefitting the Cardinals team.

THE HUNGRY, TRUCK-EATING BRIDGE

Where could you place a bet–before the casinos?

There's a railroad bridge in Charlottesville so notorious it has its very own Twitter handle (@UVAcornerbridge). Yes, it's the 14th Street Bridge, a.k.a. the Corner Bridge.

The bridge, with its clearly posted 10-foot clearance, eats rental trucks for lunch. The occurrence is so common that there's a competition among local folks to see who can most accurately pick the number of trucks that will become stuck under the bridge each year.

With a student population of about 40,000 coming and going each year, rental trucks are a common sight. A student or parent driving a rental and, perhaps, unfamiliar with the geography of the Corner, might make the terrible mistake of trying to take a more direct route through town and end up turning their leased vehicle from a moving van into a convertible.

Students: If your parent or friend starts driving toward the Corner in a box truck, let them know that 10 feet means 10 feet. There's no squeezing through. The bridge especially loves the squeezer-throughers!

Local television meteorologist Travis Koshko is the keeper of the observational contest tracking the bridge hits (winners get bragging rights only). In 2019, there were nine recorded bridge strikes; in 2020 there were five. There were more than 40 participants in the 2021 contest.

The railroad trestle at 14th Street on the Corner at UVa. Photo courtesy of @undeNIYAble.

Locals love to report on the latest victim of the bridge, snapping photos and sharing via social media.

Navigate away from the University by heading west or north, or some combination of the two. Get onto Interstate 64 or Route 29 and get far, far away from the truck-eating bridge.

TEN FEET OF CLEARANCE ON CORNER BRIDGE

WHAT: 14th Street Bridge

WHERE: The Corner, University of Virginia

COST: Your pride, if you get stuck

PRO TIP: Always measure your truck or rental before attempting a 10-foot clearance.

REAL NEAPOLITAN-STYLE PIZZA IN BELMONT

Where can you find a little bit of Naples?

Some of Charlottesville's most notable restaurants are in unassuming digs, so it's entirely possible to miss out on the best eats if you're new to town. The tiny building with the lightning bolt logo is no exception. Lampo, Charlottesville's only Neapolitan pizza joint, is something truly special. The original restaurant is so small the roof had to be opened up to drop in the authentic, wood-fired pizza oven.

From the time Lampo opened its doors, it's been a busy and growing enterprise. A takeout-only shop is under construction at IX Art Park to supplement the sit-down restaurant and its extremely limited seating.

The pizza is to die for. But don't miss out on incredible appetizers, salads, and dessert. You're going to have to go several times to work your way

REAL, NEAPOLITAN-STYLE PIZZA

WHAT: Lampo

WHERE: 205 Monticello Rd.

COST: Pizzas start at $10

PRO TIP: Lampo doesn't take reservations, and there's often a wait to get a table. Get your name on the list, wander across the street to Champion Tap Room, enjoy a beer, then wander back to claim your table when its ready. It's a winning combination.

In 2020, the restaurant donated 100% of its profits from a busy Friday to the free and reduced lunch program at the Charlottesville City Schools.

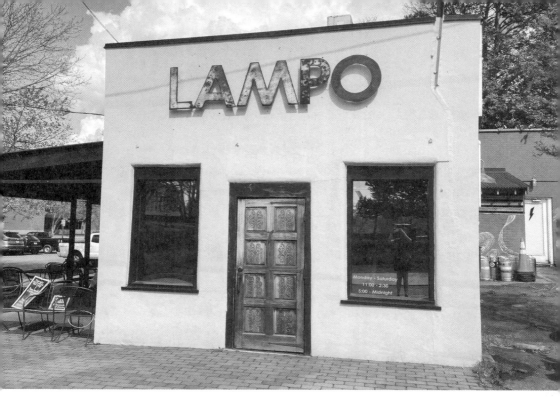

Lampo's small, yellow building in Belmont is where to find the best Neapolitan-style pizza.

all around the menu, but we recommend the Hellboy, a spicy pizza with chiles and peppered honey, and the Marinara D.O.C. If you're lucky enough to catch the eggplant Parmesan special, get that, too.

Neapolitan pizza is not for those who prefer a chain-style slice. Charred, bubbly crust is the hallmark of a true, authentic pizza. Pizza scissors are offered to guests to slice their own pies. The toppings are special, too, with some of the best sauces you'll ever experience.

TEA AND HOOKAH NOOK

What's the best place for a cozy chat and a pot of tea?

In a hidden, upstairs venue on the Downtown Mall, you'll find Charlottesville's only tea bar and hookah den. Twisted Branch Tea Bazaar attracts tea connoisseurs and hookah fans, and music fans enjoy late-night performances there as well. The atmosphere is 1960s bohemian chic, and it's the only place in town with private, curtained booths for secret whispering or silent meditation.

The crowd at Twisted Branch has come to study, work, or visit with friends. Seating is casual and cushioned with scores of pillows. The cozy outdoor patio is ideal for hookah-samplers. There's a full menu of mostly vegan and vegetarian fare for lunch or dinner, and a long list of teas and hookah flavors to explore.

It's the perfect spot to hide away and read a book on a cold winter day or to get together with a friend for some extra juicy gossip. Don't miss the full menu. Make a plan for a lunch or dinner date so you can experience, for one, the

COZY TEA ROOM

WHAT: Twisted Branch Tea Bazaar

WHERE: 414 E. Main St.

COST: Tea starts at $3.50, entrées at $7.50

PRO TIP: Join Twisted Branch's Tea Club for access to special bulk teas and guided tastings.

Alp Isin, the artist behind Budala Pottery, sells his one-of-a-kind teapots and tea-related ceramics at the shop.

Find the funky and fabulous tea bazaar in a little upstairs hideaway on the Downtown Mall.

Goatherder, an appetizer platter with pita, hummus, dolma, olives, and veggies. It's just right to pair with a pot of tea and share with a friend. If you are craving a sweet treat, the almond pave pound cake alongside a cup of masala chai can turn any frown upside down!

BOARD GAMES WITH A LOCAL CONNECTION

What's the link between Settlers and C'ville?

Have you ever played Settlers of Catan? Chances are you or someone you know has! The business of the game, now known simply as Catan, is managed right in Charlottesville by Catan Studio. With more than 27 million copies of the game sold and worldwide competitions held in Germany each year, it comes as a surprise to enthusiasts that the Catan brand is run from right here in central Virginia.

In Catan, players take the role of settlers, acquiring resources, trading, and building civilizations to earn points and win. The line of games, both physical and online, represent some of the most popular and beloved board games of the 21st century.

GAMES EVERYONE CAN PLAY

WHAT: Catan and Chickapig

WHERE: Play Chickapig at Kardinal Hall

COST: Catan, $44; Chickapig $14

NOTABLE: In the early months of 2020, during the COVID-19 pandemic, sales of Catan skyrocketed 144%.

Brian Calhoun, the creator of Chickapig, got his start making guitars for Dave Matthews, Mary Chapin Carpenter, and Keith Urban, among others.

Top: *Catan board game. Photo by Aaron Jaggers.* Inset: *Chickapig board game. Photo by Laura Byrnes. Both have local connections.*

Another game with local roots is Chickapig. With Kickstarter funding and support from the owner's friend, Dave Matthews, Chickapig is a game rapidly growing in popularity. It's fun, silly, and strategic. Its adorable cast of characters include chicken-pig hybrids, cows, and lots of cow poop, a key to game play. Kardinal Hall, a city beer garden and restaurant, hosts Chickapig Tuesdays, when guests are invited to come learn and play.

SNUGGLE A BABY GOAT

Can you handle the cuteness?

There was a time when baby goat snuggling and baby goat yoga were only known to those in the business of raising the funny little animals, but thanks to Caromont Farm, the joy of baby goats has gone mainstream.

Caromont Farm in Esmont, a short drive from Charlottesville, is a goat dairy- and cheese-making operation that supplies many of the local restaurants with their delicious products. The dairy produces more than 30,000 pounds of cheese per year!

Good cheese happens when goats are happy. To socialize baby goats and prepare them for milking, the dairy regularly puts out word, asking for volunteer goat snugglers and for those interested to take tours to learn about the cheese-making process, sample the wares, and go home with some cheese and other goat-milk products. The farm's original call for goat cuddlers went viral, making it onto

BABY GOATS

WHAT: Goat-snuggling sessions

WHERE: 9261 Old Green Mountain Rd., Esmont, VA

COST: $10 and your heart

PRO TIP: Wear your getting dirty duds and shoes; goat snuggling is not a tidy activity.

In 2016, Caromont Farms' call for volunteer goat snugglers went viral on social media, and was picked up by local, regional, and national news outlets.

Left: Baby goat. Photo by Jody Saunders. Right: Playing with goats at Caromont Farm.

national news, causing an overwhelming influx of enthusiastic goat lovers.

Planned snuggle sessions are announced online and one must make a reservation. We highly recommend the experience; adorable baby goat antics put a smile on anyone's face, and the selection of award-winning products will fill your tummy and to-go bag.

GET AROUND TOWN FOR FREE

Do you know the best way to get from town to Grounds?

Much of Charlottesville is walkable if you're in reasonably good shape and the weather cooperates. A walk from the Downtown Mall to the Rotunda at the University of Virginia is under two miles.

But sometimes you need a faster, more temperate mode of transportation. Charlottesville Area Transit (CAT) offers a free trolley to get you between the town and Grounds. The trolleys are small, dark-green buses painted to look like traditional trollies. You can hop on along the way from the Downtown Transit Station, along West Main Street, to Jefferson Park Avenue, over to Scott Stadium, through the UVa Grounds, and back to downtown. It's a great ride to get an overview of the area as you plot your next move during a Charlottesville visit.

WHERE TO CATCH THE TROLLEY

WHAT: Downtown Transit Station

WHERE: 615 Water St. E.

COST: Free

PRO TIP: Riders under 13 ride all public transportation for free. Ages 13–17 with a valid CAT ID ride for free, as well.

The trolley runs every day of the week and is a handy and free transportation option for students and townies alike. Aside

In 2016, e-scooters made their first appearance in Charlottesville. These days, Veo is the provider of dockless e-bikes and scooters, providing another rentable way to get around town.

Look for the trolley, a Charlottesville Area Transit bus in dark green, for rides between downtown and the university.

from your own two feet, it's the easiest way to get between downtown and the university.

For Charlottesville visitors, options for parking downtown can be a bit bewildering. There are, for those with parallel parking skills, a number of street options with free parking a short walk away. Beyond that, there are parking structures and surface lots where you can pay to park. But we recommend you get familiar with the streets, park and ride, or walk. There's room enough for everyone to enjoy the town and the Grounds.

LOOK AT THE SKY ABOVE

What's your best option for professionally guided stargazing?

GAZE AT THE STARS

WHAT: McCormick Observatory

WHERE: 600 McCormick Rd.

COST: Free

NOTABLE: Alvan Clark & Sons was a famous manufacturer of lenses for telescopes in the 19th and early 20th centuries. The McCormick telescope is the largest Alvan Clark refractor still mounted on its original Alvan Clark mount.

For a star-studded Friday night, head to the McCormick Observatory. The Department of Astronomy at UVa hosts open houses for the public to come and peer at the stars and planets through the McCormick and Fan Mountain telescopes.

Weather plays a significant role in the success of this outing, so it's best to check the sky and the website before heading out. If you do find the right night, the results can be spectacular. Guests are invited to peek at the sky through the facility's

Leander McCormick, for whom the Observatory is named due to his donation of the telescope, was the brother of Cyrus McCormick, who is credited with the invention of the mechanical reaper. It was, in fact, their father, Robert McCormick, who invented the reaper. Cyrus patented it and founded International Harvester.

Top: *Leander McCormick Observatory.* Inset: *Visitors look through the telescope. Photos courtesy of McCormick Observatory.*

telescopes and to experience audiovisual presentations by actual astronomers, view museum exhibits, and take guided tours of the observatory. Faculty, postdoctoral candidates, and graduate students host the open-house events and are on hand to explain what you see and to answer questions. It's a great outing for a date, a small group, or a family night. Make sure you call ahead in case the clouds will get in the way of any potential stargazing.

CHARLOTTESVILLE OLIVE GARDEN

How come there's no Olive Garden in Charlottesville?

There are an estimated 500 restaurants in the greater Charlottesville area, about 100 of these within downtown, and yet, somehow, not one of them is an Olive Garden.

For some unknown reason, the rumor of a possible Olive Garden, with its unlimited breadsticks and never-ending bowls of pasta, descending upon our fair city surfaces from time to time. There is documented interest, in Reddit topics, social media posts, and even mentions in mainstream media, with the population sharply divided. Some people really want an Olive Garden. Others simply do not.

It's weird that a run-of-the-mill chain restaurant is what people in Charlottesville might crave.

Charlottesville is not well-suited to the corporate matrix of the faux-Tuscan brand, with the corporate owner's requirement for real estate, parking, and space for diners to line up around the building

> ### CHARLOTTESVILLE'S BEST ITALIAN RESTAURANT
>
> **WHAT:** Tavola
>
> **WHERE:** 826 Hinton Ave.
>
> **COST:** Entrées start at $22
>
> **PRO TIP:** Make sure to visit Tavola's Cicchetti (small snacks) Bar, behind the restaurant. There's a separate alleyway entrance for clandestine dates.

The nearest Olive Garden is an hour's drive away in Richmond and, yes, some people make that drive to load up on all-you-can-eat pasta, salad, and breadsticks.

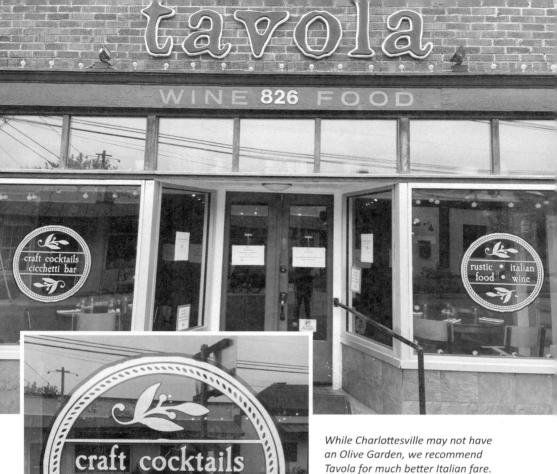

While Charlottesville may not have an Olive Garden, we recommend Tavola for much better Italian fare.

to get a table. Perhaps one day Charlottesville will rate an Olive Garden, but for now, we're just not up to their standards.

Instead, we'll point you to some of our very best Italian restaurants, with Tavola unquestionably in the number one slot, Vivace in second, and Anna's Pizza No. 5, Carmello's, and Vinny's all respectable options.

BEHIND THE SCENES AT MONTICELLO

What's the best way to see Monticello?

It's no secret that you're supposed to visit Monticello when you come to Charlottesville. About half a million people do just that every year. But a Behind-the-Scenes Day Pass reservation is a well-kept secret that allows visitors access to rooms most people never get to see. The tour is private to your group and guided by a docent through the first, second, and third floors; the big payoff is the iconic Dome Room on the third floor.

Guests learn more than ever before about the dynamics of life at Monticello, the families that lived there, and the role of enslaved people on the property. Do not miss the self-guided tour of Mulberry Row, the

A RARE GLIMPSE AT HISTORY

WHAT: Thomas Jefferson's Monticello

WHERE: 931 Thomas Jefferson Pkwy.

COST: $350 for a party of five

PRO TIP: Don't think of this as a last-minute adventure. Reservations must be made 48 hours in advance and children must be over seven years of age. The tour is not handicap-accessible. Guests must be able to climb a steep and narrow staircase unassisted.

The coolest spot to see, viewable only via the Behind-the-Scenes tour, is a small nook off the Dome Room called The Cuddy. Jefferson's granddaughters reportedly used the space as an escape from crowds of adults, and outfitted it as a small sitting room.

Top: *Monticello. Photo courtesy of Benjamin Randolph.* Inset: *Photo opportunity with Thomas Jefferson statue.*

reconstructed slave quarters, where visitors learn about the difficult lives of the enslaved families that made building and running Monticello possible.

A newer exhibit is dedicated to Sally Hemings, a slave of Thomas Jefferson who also was his mistress and mother of some of his children. Before the year 2000 or so, visitors to Monticello heard only a brief mention of Sally Hemings. Now, visitors learn much about the Hemings family and how their lives were linked with Jefferson's for generations.

SERPENTINE WALLS

Why are there gardens behind walls?

A stroll around the Grounds at UVa will reveal numerous Pavilion Gardens enclosed by gates and serpentine brick walls. While these gardens look like private property, they're not. Open to the public, the back Pavilion Gardens are gorgeous, meticulously kept spaces, so feel free to step through gates and poke around.

The serpentine walls are the site of numerous graduation and wedding photo shoots. Originally, though, the walls were constructed to hide from the rest of the community at the university the view of the scores of enslaved laborers going about their daily work. The walls kept the livestock in and the deer and foxes out. The enclosures were where the butchering was done, the food was made, and the laundry was boiled and hung to dry. A whole community of hundreds of enslaved men, women, and children

---

IF THESE WALLS COULD TALK

WHAT: Pavilion Gardens

WHERE: University of Virginia

COST: Free

NOTABLE: John Patten Emmet (1796–1842) was the chair of the School of Natural History at UVa, where he lectured on chemistry, botany, geology, mineralogy, and zoology. Interest in Emmet and his early experiments has resurfaced, with the discovery of a hidden chemical hearth in the wall of the Rotunda's Lower East Oval Room.

Emmet previously occupied Pavilion I, where he dabbled in zoology. He collected snakes, an owl, and even a bear before building the home he's associated with, Morea, which still stands on Sprigg Lane.

Don't miss the hidden Pavilion Gardens behind serpentine walls at the University of Virginia. They're open to the public, and each one is different.

worked and lived within the enclosures.

No two gardens are alike, so take a look at each as you tour on foot.

At the end of Sprigg Lane lies Morea, a true secret garden and arboretum established by John Patten Emmet in the 1830s. Emmet, appointed by Thomas Jefferson as the university's first professor of natural history, collected mulberry, coffee, and orange trees to grow in his garden. In the 1960s, The Albemarle Garden Club added hollies and other native plants.

UNDER THE BLUE RIDGE

Are you afraid of the dark?

If you like exploring in the dark, have we got the experience for you! The recently opened Blue Ridge Tunnel Trail is the best dark-as-midnight daytime adventure. You absolutely must have a flashlight, headlamp, bike light, or other trusty illumination. The tunnel is nearly a mile long, making it impossible to see end-to-end. Bright lights will enable you to see the plant life and creatures that enjoy the damp, underground life. Keep an eye out for frogs and salamanders!

There are two official parking areas to reach the tunnel. They fill up fast, so for the best results, plan your hike (or bike) of the tunnel early in the day. The eastern end is at the Afton Depot off of US Route 6, and it's a 15-minute hike to reach the eastern tunnel entrance. This is the more polished tunnel entrance, with quicker access from the parking area.

The western tunnel access is off US Route 250 West toward Waynesboro from the interstate turnoff. The hike from the parking area is rather long and hilly, so if you're traveling with young kids or physically challenged folks, you may wish to choose the eastern access instead. Hike or bike through and back to return to your parking area of choice.

In the planning and construction of the original tunnel, Claudius Crozet's calculations were so accurate that when

A ONE-OF-A KIND HIKE

WHAT: Blue Ridge Tunnel Trail

WHERE: West Trailhead: 483 Three Notched Mountain Hwy.; Waynesboro, VA; East Trailhead: 215 Afton Depot Ln., Afton, VA.

COST: Free

PRO TIP: Bring flashlights or headlamps and make sure you have fresh batteries. Wear waterproof shoes or hiking boots, as you're likely to get muddy.

154

Scenes from the mile-long, newly completed Blue Ridge Tunnel Trail. Photos by Hunter Chorey.

the crews approaching from either end met, only "one-half-inch separated their alignment." Crozet, a town in Albemarle County, is named for Claudius Crozet, a French educator, soldier, and civil engineer, and one of the founding members of Virginia Military Institute.

At the time of the tunnel's completion in 1858, the 4,273-foot Blue Ridge Tunnel was the longest tunnel in the United States. It took nine years to complete. A documentary called *The Tunnel* reveals the story of its creation and the work of Irish immigrants and enslaved African Americans.

ART TO EXPERIENCE

Is that a giant butt?

You might discover IX by accident while on a quest for tacos that takes you to Brazos or in search of sake at North American Sake Company. You enter the parking area and admire the flowers, the ivy-covered dome, and the works of art on every surface. Then you notice something quite different.

Behold the giant tattooed butt, the Love Butt, a 1,600-pound sculpture that was donated by a comedian after the large rear made its debut on a television pilot and then was no longer needed. Today it serves as a backdrop for ridiculous selfies.

Beyond the butt, there's much to see at IX Art Park. Explore the many sculptures, murals, photography exhibits, paintings, and pathways. There's always something new to discover.

An outdoor stage hosts a variety of musical events. Indoors, you'll find The Rabbit Hole, an indoor event venue and art gallery, in addition to The Looking Glass, an immersive art experience.

ART IN PLACE

WHAT: IX Art Park

WHERE: 522 Second St. S.E.

COST: Free

PRO TIP: IX hosts numerous events; stay on top of the activities by subscribing to the newsletter available through ixartpark.org.

The space was the former site of the Frank Ix and Sons textile factory. The concrete-and-steel warehouse and its surroundings were all but abandoned when it was redeveloped in 2014. Owner Ludwig Kuttner had a vision to turn the space into a vibrant, engaging, inviting property and worked with a team of like-minded people to create the ever-evolving project.

The Art Park itself is free and open to the public. The Looking Glass, The Rabbit Hole and the events held there are ticketed, but affordable.

Sculptures, photo exhibits, art, and the stage are just some of what visitors see at IX Art Park.

Supported in part by grants from the National Endowment of the Arts and the Virginia Commission for the Arts, IX Art Park is a 501(c)3 that aims to remain affordable to a multigenerational, multicultural audience. IX provides support for numerous artists by providing a platform for them to share their work. The Art Park is host to more than 250 events per year.

Ludwig Kuttner and his wife, the artist and style icon Beatrix Ost, are two of Charlottesville's most interesting characters. Beatrix is one of the contributing artists of The Looking Glass. With her inimitable style, purple hair, and, well, presence, she's impossible to miss and is often seen walking her two enormous hounds downtown.

NATURE, PRESERVED

Where can you explore nature and the African American Heritage Trail?

A quick six miles north of the city of Charlottesville and half a mile from the intersection of Hydraulic and West Rio roads is Ivy Creek Natural Area. Ivy Creek is a 216-acre preserve, surprisingly easy to reach and a delightful surprise. The property is along the South Fork Rivanna River Reservoir and provides seven miles of easy to moderate hiking trails. There is a 3/4-mile trail that is wheelchair-accessible.

Hiking at Ivy Creek gives visitors the varied experience of walking through meadows, along shoreline, through woods, and over streams. As a natural area, no dogs are allowed, and rules for protecting the environment are strictly enforced.

An official site on the Virginia African American Heritage Trail, the land was purchased by Hugh Carr, a formerly enslaved man, in 1870, and used as a family farm. Known then as River View Farm, the land remained in the Carr and Greer families

Ivy Creek was very nearly a 200-home subdivision. Following the death of her parents, Evangeline Greer sold the property. Charlottesville and Albemarle County stepped in and purchased the land to prevent that development from happening.

Top: *Barred owl. Photo courtesy of Bob Gore.* Inset: *Barn. Photo courtesy of Rochelle Garwood.*

for more than 100 years before becoming Ivy Creek Natural Area.

Carr's daughter, Mary Carr Greer, for whom Greer Elementary School is named, became an influential educator in the region, a principal of Albemarle Training School, and the initiator of high school curriculum for African American students in the region. Mary and her husband, Conley Greer, purchased River View Farm from Mary's father, and after Mary's death the estate worked with The Nature Conservancy on a plan to create the Ivy Creek Natural Area we enjoy today.

There's plenty to learn in the educational buildings on-site, featuring exhibits and programming events. Ivy Creek makes for an ideal field trip, or just an excellent place to take a peaceful walk.

COLD WAR MILITARY BUNKERS

What's beneath Peters Mountain?

About 130 miles away from Charlottesville in White Sulphur Springs, West Virginia, there is a bunker built beneath the Greenbrier Resort. A relic of the Cold War, the Greenbrier Bunker was meant to house all 535 members of Congress in the event of a nuclear war. The bunker is no longer a secret; in fact, visitors take tours of the space regularly.

It should be no surprise that other areas within a short drive of Washington, DC, have also seen the development of military bunkers, some within range of Charlottesville and all very much still secret.

The Peters Mountain Facility, 16 miles north of Charlottesville, has long been fodder for conspiracy theorists. It is a guarded space with road closure signs protecting it and a high fence surrounding the grounds. The land is owned by AT&T and includes a helicopter pad and several satellite dishes, all observable from the air.

But what is it?

Sources say that the site is home to a hub for government continuity planning: a bunker capable of housing several hundred people that could serve as a relocation site for an intelligence agency

---

In the event of an attack, it's unlikely that key government officials would have time to travel as far as just outside Charlottesville, Virginia. That's why rumors of a secure, underground bunker, possibly a five-story, self-contained facility accessible via tunnel from the Oval Office, are probably true.

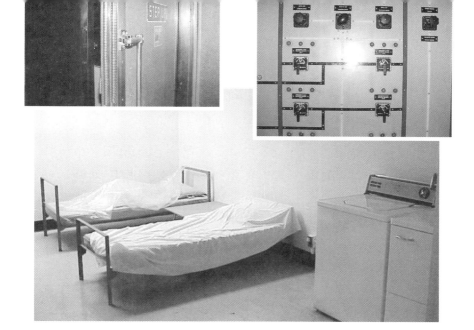

Top left: *Shielded doors in Cold War-era bunker.* Top right: *Control panel.* Bottom: *Buckingham station. Photos courtesy of Roger Voisinet.*

in the event of an attack on the US Capital. Home to an AT&T communications station (aerial photos show an AT&T logo painted on a helipad), the secret site may very well be a decommissioned Cold War holdover, like the Greenbrier facility.

SECRET UNDERGROUND BUNKER

WHAT: The Peters Mountain Facility

WHERE: On the border between Alleghany County, VA, Monroe County, WV, Giles County., VA, and Craig County, VA.

COST: Free to wonder about. Trespassing is illegal.

NOTABLE: Garrett M. Graff authored the book *Raven Rock*, a history of continuity-of-government programs in the United States. His book shares more about the Peters Mountain facility, both historically and now.

GET IN SOME STEPS

Looking for a stroller-friendly hike?

The gravel paths and boardwalk bridges of the two-mile trek up Monticello Mountain make for an ideal hike for walkers of all capabilities. The Saunders-Monticello Trail is scenic and friendly.

Walking all the way to the top gets you to the David M. Rubenstein Visitor Center at Monticello, in case you need a pit stop. An up-and-back run is a seriously strenuous workout.

This trail, with its views of the Blue Ridge Mountains and boardwalks over deep ravines, is mostly shady in the summer, making it the ideal hike for hot days. The gravel paths are great when other hikes might be too muddy to traverse.

Grounds crews meticulously maintain the trails, closing them to visitors between dusk and dawn and when conditions can be slick or dangerous. This is among the many reasons the Saunders-Monticello Trail is so popular.

GOOD PLACE FOR A STROLL

WHAT: Saunders-Monticello Trail

WHERE: 931 Thomas Jefferson Pkwy.

COST: Free

PRO TIP: With a maximum 5% grade incline, Saunders-Monticello Trail is great for strollers, wheelchairs, and walkers who need an easier stroll. Leashed dogs are allowed on the lower trails, but not on the upper boardwalks.

If you're in the mood for an off-trail stroll, Monticello's Secluded Farm trails are an excellent addition to the experience, best suited to a dry, seasonal day good for wandering the woods in their natural state.

Gravel trails and boardwalks make the Saunders-Monticello Trail easy and more accessible. Don't miss the overlooks and rustic trails.

There are two parking areas; one is small and located on Thomas Jefferson Parkway. It often is full to overflowing. If that's the case, exit the lot, turn left, then right back onto State Route 20, and take the next right onto Dairy Barn Road, where there's a much larger parking lot. From this lot, the trail goes through an underpass tunnel to enter the park and trail area.

URBAN HIKING ADVENTURES

Where can you hop on an urban hiking trail?

You might catch a glimpse here and there of a dark green, diamond-shaped insignia on the side of the road, across from a parking lot, or behind a baseball diamond. Let your feet follow your curiosity to the Rivanna Trail, a 20-plus-mile urban trail that loops around and through city sites.

The Rivanna Trail is an urban wilderness hiking trail built and maintained by volunteers that loops around the city of Charlottesville and includes sections that range from easy to strenuous. The trail meanders by and sometimes over creeks, streams, and rivers. The trail is only continuous if you're willing to do a few slight off-trail jogs over city roads, through waterways (sometimes with stepping stones), or through some soggy, muddy spots. Some of our favorite hikes include an out-and-back section of the trail, rather than trying to do the whole loop in a day.

Along the way, you'll experience gentle streams, steep climbs, sweet bridges across waterways, open meadows, backyard views, parks and ballfields, highway glimpses, graffitied underpasses, and much more.

The Rivanna Trail is a community-wide treasure for exercise, relaxation, and nature-related education. With several access

The Free State Trail, a spur of the Rivanna Trail, runs from between Locust Avenue and Holmes Avenue north through Pen Park and the Dunlora and Belvedere neighborhoods. In 1788, Amy Bowles Farrow, a free woman of color, bought 224 acres of land that is where those neighborhoods are now. Once known as Free State, the area was one of the earliest free Black communities in Virginia.

Scenes from along the Rivanna Trail. Top left and top right: Photos courtesy of Jennifer Alluisi.

URBAN HIKING

WHAT: Rivanna Trail

WHERE: Under, around, and through the city of Charlottesville

COST: Free

PRO TIP: The trail is not yet continuous. Hikers may find it necessary to travel across roadways or streams to take detours to pick up the trail in its next available location.

points, the trail connects many neighborhoods and six city parks. It is open for hiking and jogging from sunup to sundown. Most of the trail passes over private property, so hikers are asked to stay on the trail and keep dogs on leashes at all times. Trail guides are available at visitors' centers, at local outdoor and running stores, and on the Rivanna Trail website.

Once a month, the Rivanna Trail Foundation hosts a work party, which is a gathering of volunteers to tackle the creation of bridges and paths, to create new sections of trail, and to clear and make safer the existing paths.

GAS STATION GOODIES

What's your favorite fudge flavor?

The Crossroad Corner Store is full of surprises. What looks like a simple gas station and convenience store from the outside has much more to offer inside. One friend said that during the holiday season, their family likes to begin at Dr. Ho's Humble Pie in North Garden for some of the best pizza and salads in the whole region. After the family places their order, they send the kids next door to the Crossroad Corner Store with cash to buy gifts and stocking stuffers for each other—a genius idea.

Homemade pies and cakes, many varieties of fudge, breakfast, and a hot lunch are served at the store Monday through Saturday. A glass case holds enormous slabs of cake, chocolate eclairs, and fancy cream pies.

Tables in the back allow guests to enjoy their meal in peace and take a gander at the family and guest photos that line the walls. If you're exploring your touristy options, there's a full array of brochures for events spanning the area.

If you find yourself south of town, the two musts are Dr. Ho's for pizza and a visit to the Crossroad Store for an unexpected find.

NORTH GARDEN CONVENIENCE STORE

WHAT: Crossroad Corner Store

WHERE: 4916 Plank Rd., North Garden, VA

COST: $5 will get you any number of goodies at the Crossroad Corner Store.

PRO TIP: Don't miss the Christmas tree lighting, a celebrated community event in North Garden, in the area next to the parking lot that serves Dr. Ho's and the Corner Store.

Top: *Crossroad Store.* Bottom: *Gift shop.* Inset: *Dr. Ho's Pizza.* More than anyone expects from a convenience store.

The Hambsch family owned the entire Crossroad complex at one time. Now, they own Loving Cup Vineyard and Winery, well-known for their organic wines.

A HISTORY WALK WITH A GHOSTLY SPIN

Do you believe in ghosts?

One of the wildest stories locals love to share is about the Charlottesville mayor who killed his wife. J. Samuel McCue allegedly shot and killed his wife, Fannie Crawford McCue, on September 4, 1904, at their home on Park Street.

The house, a striking building at 501 Park Street, is now occupied by Hospice of the Piedmont.

McCue was executed for the crime, and the rope that was supposedly used in the hanging is kept in the archives of the Alderman Library at the University of Virginia. Well-documented in the *Daily Progress*, the crime was reported as one of rage, in which the mayor sought to silence his wife's complaints about his association with other women. The former mayor sought to get away with the homicide, placing a call to police with a story about burglars, and telling an elaborate tale about the burglars shooting Mrs. McCue then assaulting Sam McCue and leaving him for dead.

The former mayor maintained his innocence throughout the investigation, even placing an ad in the newspaper and offering a reward for the capture of the true murderers.

A downtown walking tour invites participants to take on the roles of Sam and Frannie McCue. The tour uses landmarks to

A popular activity for corporate outings, Tell Me About It Tours once hosted all the managers from the Charlottesville-based State Farm office and included custom content about the ghost who haunts their corporate offices.

The Albemarle County Historical Society building is a treasure trove of historic books and artifacts; visitors enjoy a tour of Court Square.

GHOSTLY DOWNTOWN TOURS

WHAT: Tell Me About It Tours

WHERE: Downtown, weekends in October and online anytime.

COST: $150 for a private tour of six or fewer, $10 for the online version.

PRO TIP: See the rope used to hang Sam McCue in the University of Virginia Alderman Library Archives.

share the stories of the city and Albemarle County.

The tour, hosted by storyteller and historian Rob Craighurst of Tell Me About It Tours, makes 24 stops over two hours, and is a great way to gain familiarity with downtown streets and sights, including the Park Street mansion where the murder took place.

Craighurst says that the tour is fun for all ages, and guests often end up sharing ghost stories from their own experiences. The story told raises all kinds of questions about criminal justice, the death penalty, and witness testimony. Many find that there's lots to think and talk about once the tour is over.

Not too spooky, the tour is fun and educational, and focuses on solving the mystery behind the murder.

HORSING AROUND

Can you play a game on a horse?

Virginia is known for many sports, and the university's basketball and football programs get a lot of attention. But there's another Friday Night Lights sport that spectators enjoy, especially if you like horses! Virginia Polo hosts exhibition matches most Fridays at their facility, just five miles from the university Grounds, south of town off of Old Lynchburg Road. The idyllic setting, with a view of the Blue Ridge Mountains and neighboring Biscuit Run State Park, is a lovely place to watch an exciting game of polo.

Virginia Polo is a student-run, nonprofit organization that teaches University of Virginia students to play and compete. There are additional programs for high school-aged, aspiring polo players, and leagues of local adults that use the facilities for games as well.

POLO IN CHARLOTTESVILLE

WHAT: Virginia Polo Club

WHERE: 1082 Forest Lodge Ln.

COST: Free

PRO TIP: Spectators and competitors are discouraged from bringing dogs to the facility. Any dog brought needs to be leashed at all times.

The facilities are top-notch, with both an indoor and outdoor arena for exhibitions, fields for the resident horses to romp, stables, and a building for special events. There are no concessions, however so if you come as a spectator, bring your own drinks and snacks.

Student members are assigned to care for and feed the horses, so, outside of exhibition time, horses are tended and exercised in preparation for the big day.

UVa Club and Varsity games are scheduled on Fridays during the fall and winter seasons. Guests are invited to tailgate outside the arena.

WISEHART

Meet the polo ponies and enjoy top-notch polo facilities with a gorgeous view. If you can, catch a match with the national champion UVa Women's Polo Team.

Polo matches happen off-site, too. It's not uncommon to find polo at King Family Winery during the summer months, with the Virginia Polo Club participating in these events. If you happen to catch a winery match and feel like you want more polo in your life, Virginia Polo Club is just the ticket. If you think polo is the sport for you, summertime programs are offered for locals to learn about and become part of the polo community.

LITTLE FREE LIBRARIES

Where can you get a free book, curbside?

There are more than 16 Little Free Libraries scattered throughout the Charlottesville-Albemarle region. In 2009, a man named Todd Bol created the first little library in his front yard in Hudson, Wisconsin. Little did he know that his take-a-book, leave-a-book idea would become a widespread social enterprise, with more than 100,000 registered Little Free Libraries worldwide.

Jane Belisle has one of Charlottesville's very first little curbside libraries. She says she was enchanted by the idea when she first saw the book-filled boxes on a trip to Portland, Oregon, and decided that for her birthday, she would buy, register, and decorate her very own.

Being a steward of a Little Free Library means registering with the organization's network, which allows people to easily find the book boxes. There are resources for stewards in the network, and your library might be featured in the organization's communications or social media outreach!

Stewards keep their boxes filled either by encouraging contributions, or by stocking up from library sales or other resources. Jane says that magazines go fast in the summer, when people stock up for poolside reads.

The next phase of the movement may be Little Free Pantries, like the mini pantry at First and Oak streets, where the stewards and friends stock up on canned goods, dried pasta, breakfast cereals, and anything else that might be helpful to someone who is hungry or in need.

Right: *Little free library on Lexington Avenue. Photo courtesy of Jane Belisle.* Inset: *Little free library at Johnson Elementary. Photo courtesy of Rebecca Flowers.*

BOOK BORROWING

WHAT: Little Free Libraries

WHERE: littlefreelibrary.org/ourmap to find all Charlottesville locations

COST: Free, or $250 to start a registered library of your own.

PRO TIP: Be thoughtful with your library donations. Stewards prefer clean books in reasonably good condition in a variety of genres.

It's been several years since Jane's popular neighborhood library was founded, and it has given her great joy. She says that her favorite visitors are a dad and daughter who come, select a book, and sit right down on the curb to read it before heading home.

Have you donated or selected a book from a Little Free Library?

MURALS ALL OVER TOWN

Where can you learn more about the art around town?

There are more than 40 murals around Charlottesville! It's a challenge to find them all, so make a day of it and conduct a mural scavenger hunt. Most are outdoors and are easily seen by the public. Others are indoors, and you have to know where to go to find them.

Enter the Charlottesville Mural Project. The Bridge Progressive Arts Initiative is behind this enterprise, putting together properties willing to host the artwork and the artists interested in creating it. To make it easy, the initiative has created a map on its website with a suggested two-mile mural walk, a seven-mile bike loop, and ways to ride public transportation to see many of the works of art.

Some of the more visible works include *Together We Grow*, a collaborative effort from designer/artist Jake Van Yahres, painter Christy Baker, and students from Charlottesville High School. This mural, which

ART IN ALL THE PLACES

WHAT: Charlottesville Mural Project

WHERE: Find locations at Charlottesvillemuralproject.org/map

COST: Free

PRO TIP: Take one of the organization's recommended bike tours to see several murals in a seven-mile loop.

The *Freedom of Speech Wall* is a monument on the Downtown Mall. This ever-changing mural is created over and over through contributors using the available chalk to write and draw. The wall is washed weekly so that new art and messages can appear.

Take a walking tour to see Old Cheyenne, *a hidden Main Street mural* (right), *an undersea mural across from the railroad tracks near First Street* (left), *and the ever-changing mural at the Freedom of Expression wall* (bottom).

depicts trees as people holding hands, appears on the side of the Violet Crown Theater building.

The *I Love Charlottesville A Lot* mural is iconic. Frequently photographed and the backdrop of thousands of visitor selfies, the artwork is on the side of an automotive shop in Belmont. The Os in the words are used tires!

The *Charlottesville Bikes* mural appears on the concrete wall that lines the walkway on West Market Street.

See if you can find them all!

EDIBLE LANDSCAPING

Where can you sample while you shop?

Part landscaping store and part paradise, the plant-lined paths at Edible Landscaping are great for a stroll and to sample the goods. Just outside of Charlottesville in bucolic Afton, shoppers can wander rows of fragrant, flowering fruit trees and taste what's in season. Explore varieties of plant and shrubs you've never considered calling your own. Learn from experts what grows well in the local climate and how best to plant, nurture, and care for your purchases.

Don't bother with lunch if you go in the summertime. Instead, snack on blueberries, strawberries, apples, and peaches, right from their stems. No herbicides are used on Edible Landscaping's plants, and the shop prides itself on not having any plant derived from genetically modified organisms.

GARDEN TOUR

WHAT: Edible Landscaping

WHERE: 361 Spirit Ridge Ln., Afton, VA

COST: Free to browse

PRO TIP: Sign up for a volunteer day and help with weeding, pruning, and other tasks. Volunteers earn $10/hour credit for future purchases.

You'll be entranced by the property. And if you're not already convinced you have a green thumb, the staff will show you the way. Come to learn and buy, and leave enchanted.

Edible Landscaping wants all its customers to be successful with their purchases. Online and in-person workshops help even the most novice gardener.

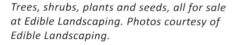

Trees, shrubs, plants and seeds, all for sale at Edible Landscaping. Photos courtesy of Edible Landscaping.

A short drive from the landscaping paradise is another Afton favorite: Afton Mountain Vineyards. Their award-winning wines and spectacular views are a great follow-up to garden browsing, and the perfect way to wind up an afternoon in the Virginia countryside.

HONOR FALLEN FIREFIGHTERS

Where do we honor the victims of tragedy?

The fire station at Fontaine has a very special monument on display. In an area visible to passersby and open to the public, the Charlottesville fire station has created a memorial to the victims of 9/11. Invited to visit New York City in the aftermath of the collapse of the World Trade Center, Charlottesville firefighters selected a large steel beam from the collection of artifacts from the site. The beam has FDNY spray-painted on it in several places. The markings indicate that four fallen firefighters were trapped and lost their lives in close proximity to the steel.

The Charlottesville fire chief selected the beam and made a commitment to the memorial

FIREFIGHTERS 9/11 MEMORIAL

WHAT: Fontaine Fire Station

WHERE: 2420 Fontaine Ave.

COST: Free

NOTABLE: 2,977 victims were killed in the September 11, 2001, attacks. These included 343 firefighters (including a chaplain and two paramedics) of the New York City Fire Department (FDNY).

There's another 9/11 memorial in Charlottesville: at UVa, another piece of World Trade Center steel is on display in Newcomb Hall. During the dedication, a flag that flew over the U.S. Capitol was given to the family of Glenn Davis Kirwin, a UVa alumnus and victim of the 9/11 attack.

Top: *Steel beam from the 9/11 wreckage of the World Trade Center in New York City.* Inset: *Charlottesville Fire Department Fontaine Avenue Fire Station. Photos courtesy of Charlottesville Fire Department.*

as a way of honoring those firefighters and all the first responders who lost their lives on September 11, 2001. In addition to the steel beam, the memorial includes a stone from the Pentagon wreckage, an American flag from the Pentagon, and a memorial stone from the Flight 93 crash in Pennsylvania.

Visitors can pay their respects in the fire station's lobby, which is lined with photographs of firefighters working amid the World Trade Center rubble, a truly moving exhibit.

CHICKEN STRIP

Do you like fried chicken?

If fried chicken is your favorite meal, Charlottesville is a good place for you to be. We have it all, from chain-restaurant chicken to fancy, highfalutin-restaurant chicken, to the best gas-station fare.

There's a stretch of road in town locals sometimes refer to as Chicken Strip that hosts a KFC, a Raising Cane's, and a Popeye's—all in incredibly close proximity. And you don't have to go far to get to a Chick-fil-A!

Fried chicken, a staple of the South, is on the menu at Michie Tavern, where we're sure the poultry's been frying since the historic tavern was established in 1784.

Locals will direct you posthaste away from the tourist-crowded tavern and clear of Chicken Strip to the tiny, unassuming Wayside Chicken, Brown's, or the GoCo Food Mart for authentic, Southern-fried chicken at a bargain price, to take out and take home, served with sweet tea and a side of potato salad. Wayside seems to be the fan favorite of fried poultry enthusiasts.

FRIED CHICKEN IN CHARLOTTESVILLE

WHAT: Wayside Takeout and Catering

WHERE: 2203 Jefferson Park Ave.

COST: A family deal will run you about $20.

PRO TIP: Lots of the chicken served in Charlottesville restaurants is locally sourced. You can always ask where your chicken originated.

Top and bottom left: *Wayside Chicken, the number-one favorite fried-chicken joint.* Bottom right: *Signs for KFC, Popeye's, and Raising Cane's are all in a row on what locals call Chicken Strip.*

It's legal to raise chickens inside city limits. In fact, there's a Charlottesville League of Chicken Keepers (CLUCK).

PEEK AT THE FARM

Where can General Custer find his boots?

In the Locust Grove neighborhood is an old, historic, property. Currently called The Farm and formerly known as Lewis Farm, the land previously was owned by Nicholas Meriwether beginning in 1735.

In 1825, University of Virginia professor of law John A.G. Davis purchased part of the 1,000-acre-plus property and hired Thomas Jefferson's proteges William Phillips and Malcolm Clark to design—and used enslaved laborers to build—the house that remains.

Civil War commander General George Armstrong Custer was stationed there in March of 1865. In 1998, a group of Custer enthusiasts (are they perhaps called Custer'ds?) presented the current resident with a pair of the general's boots, which are still kept at the house as a conversation piece.

HISTORICALLY PROTECTED PROPERTY

WHAT: The Farm

WHERE: 1201 Jefferson St. E.

COST: Free to see from the outside; not open to the public.

NOTABLE: The house, built in 1826 on the property, is considered to be one of the best surviving examples of Jeffersonian residential architecture.

Students at the University of Virginia were rioting in the fall of 1840 over the right to bear arms while attending the college. During one such riot, professor John A.G. Davis was shot and killed by a student.

Top: *The Farm.* Left inset: *National Register of Historic Places marker.* Right inset: *The house where General Custer was once stationed.*

The Daughters of the American Revolution claim that Daniel Boone was imprisoned at The Farm, but there's no proof of this. It's more likely that the boots actually belonged to Custer than it is that Daniel Boone rested there. We may never know!

FRY'S SPRING BEACH CLUB: PRIVATE CLUB MAKING AMENDS

Where can you take a dip in a pool with a history?

The history of private and even public swimming pools in the United States is one of racism and segregation.

The history of Fry's Spring Beach Club (FSBC) is similar to that of other private clubs. Founded in 1921, FSBC was popular among white elites. In the post-World War II era, the club was the only venue with a liquor license, making it, no doubt, one of the most popular venues in town. The swimming component was strong, too, with the Jefferson Swim League getting its start there, ready to grow into the one of the largest sports organizations in central Virginia.

Following *Brown v. Board of Education* (1954), public swimming pools desegregated, but private clubs were not required to do so, and FSBC was among those that continued its all-white membership policy. It wasn't until the club changed hands in 1968 that the policy was changed and the club became integrated.

To its credit, FSBC does not shy away from confronting its racist past. As part of the club's 100th anniversary, its board of directors made a commitment to inclusivity and community outreach. FSBC is working with community

SWIM CLUB AND MORE!

WHAT: Fry's Spring Beach Club

WHERE: 2512 Jefferson Park Ave.

COST: Memberships begin at $423 (individual, voting) and go up to $1,038 (family, non-voting)

PRO TIP: Families spend whole summer days around the pool, and the Champion Brewing Company–run concession stand does much to contribute to that, with a full menu of snacks, meals, and adult beverages for the grownups.

A summer day at Fry's Spring Beach Club.

partners, such as the Equity Center at the University of Virginia, to make its pools and green spaces more accessible and to welcome to the club families with children who might not otherwise have access to a pool in the summer months.

As a private club, FSBC hosts open-house events for the public to explore interest in membership. If you're invited by a member and get the opportunity to attend a public event there, go! The green spaces, the tree canopy, and the well-maintained swimming pools make the club one of the finest places to be during Virginia's hottest days of the year.

Member families are invited to sponsor other families or contribute toward children's summer camp or swim team fees in support of FSBC's initiatives to increase the ethnic, racial, and socioeconomic diversity of the club's membership and staff.

THE EXTRAS AT MONTPELIER

Where can you see the dramatic restoration of an historic home?

The drive up to James Madison's Montpelier is full of rolling hills and Blue Ridge vistas. When you arrive at the estate, you're greeted with a fine view of the Montpelier estate. It's a great, historic tour, and everyone should put it on their to-do list.

Today, Montpelier is more than the home of James Madison, fourth president of the United States. It is a memorial to enslaved people, with a rich, engaging exhibit demonstrating that history and a museum of American history.

Because of its time-capsule quality, be sure to pop into the duPont Room, located in the visitor's center. A reproduction of the decorating style of the era when the duPont family owned the mansion, the room has been re-created in full Art Deco style, complete with photographs of the duPont family's equestrian collection. Marion duPont Scott was the last private owner of the estate. Upon her demise in 1983, she bequeathed Montpelier to the National Trust for Historic Preservation. An excellent video shown in the on-site theater gives a great overview of the restoration of the property and ongoing efforts to return its rooms to their Madison-era glory.

Madison died in a room in the house, as your tour guide will share, and is buried on the estate, in case you care to pay your respects.

Top: *James Madison's Montpelier. Photo courtesy of Ron Cogswell.* Inset: *Walking trails at Montpelier.*

TIME CAPSULE

WHAT: James Madison's Montpelier

WHERE: 11350 Constitution Hwy., Montpelier Station, VA

COST: $32/adult

PRO TIP: Use the excuse of the drive to Orange, VA to continue exploring the area, including a visit to Barboursville Vineyards for award-winning wines and the Barboursville Ruins, the remains of a mansion on the property.

Allow extra time in your visit to fully explore the eight-mile trail system through the old-growth James Madison Landmark Forest, fields of wildflowers, and horse pastures. The trails allow for education in nature, and are a lovely complement to the visit.

If you visit in the autumn, the Fall Fiber Festival with its arts and crafts vendors and sheepdog trials is an absolute must.

THE SECRET TO GREAT LOCAL FISHING

Are you an aspiring angler?

Maybe you're new to fishing or are just a casual, vacation-only angler. If your interest in fishing runs deeper than that, a membership in the area's most exclusive fishing club might be everything you dream of.

Fishing guide service and pro shop, Albemarle Angler, offers memberships called Sachem's Pass, with four levels of membership. Those who buy in gain access to local private waters for the best fishing available locally.

At the highest levels of membership, the annual Sachem's Pass, members get four guided fishing trips per year. Some levels include parking passes and necessary equipment, as well as members-only discounts on

THE SECRET TO GREAT FISHING

WHAT: Albemarle Angler

WHERE: 1129 Emmet St. N.

COST: Annual memberships range in price from $1,500 to $3,000.

PRO TIP: If fishing is your favorite recreational activity, take a look at the international tours available via Albemarle Angler, with guides accompanying anglers to Cuba, Mexico, Belize, and elsewhere. albemarleangler.com.

Sponsors of the annual members' oyster roast include Starr Hill Brewery and Potter's Craft Cider, two local companies that support local water sports.

Albemarle Angler guides provide access to great fishing on private water. Photos courtesy of Albemarle Angler.

apparel and equipment available exclusively in the storefront location of the Albemarle Angler Shop in the Barracks Road Shopping Center.

The club has the benefit of camaraderie as well, gathering members annually for a big oyster roast, where local anglers can gather to share their fish tales and plot their future plans on the water.

SOURCES

The "In" Crowd news.virginia.edu/content/he-retires-sandy-gilliam-answers-14-your-questions-uva-history; tribune.com.pk/story/1785660/ignorance-prejudice-learning-kofi-annan; en.wikipedia.org/wiki/Secret_societies_at_the_University_of_Virginia; nationalgeographic.com/travel/intelligent-travel/2012/05/10/secret-societies-in-charlottesville

The Central Eyesore zilog80.com; dailyprogress.com/news/local/long-languishing-downtown-mall-building-gets-new-name-again/article_3a95675b-1cd8-5e5a-b294-337db8b91405.html; c-ville.com/signer-fed-eyesore-called-landmark; c-ville.com/mall-rats-does-the-downtown-mall-have-a-rodent-problem

Dead Poet Society cvillepedia.org/Edgar_Allan_Poe; news.virginia.edu/content/university-virginia-spirit-poe-resides-evermore; aig.alumni.virginia.edu/raven; poemuseum.org/poe-in-richmond

Crash Site on Bucks Elbow Mountain en.wikipedia.org/wiki/Piedmont_Airlines_Flight_349; readthehook.com/83798/cover-alone-mountain-true-story-flight-349; solesurvivor.info; amazon.com/Sole-survivor-Piedmont-Flight-Mountain/dp/B0006FCIVS; crozetgazette.com/2013/09/07/piedmont-flight-349-sole-survivor-phil-bradley-dies-at-87

Home to the Grand Duchess of Russia en.wikipedia.org/wiki/Execution_of_the_Romanov_family; en.wikipedia.org/wiki/Anna_Anderson; readthehook.com/86004/cover-jack-amp-anna-remembering-czar-charlottesville-eccentrics; dailyprogress.com/125yearsofprogress/anastasia-abducted-from-charlottesville-hospital-this-day-in-1983/article_5e38d7a2-d48b-11e7-b5fe-0bcb4c84f922.html

Art and Poetry on the Corner en.wikipedia.org/wiki/Rita_Dove; news.virginia.edu/content/mural-brings-poet-laureate-professors-work-life-uvas-corner; people.virginia.edu/~rfd4b; blogs.loc.gov/catbird/2019/12/rita-dove-and-on-the-bus-with-rosa-parks

Jazz for Charity c-ville.com/area-musicians-get-jazzed-albemarle-high-school-benefit

Nature, Play, and Discovery cvilletomorrow.org/articles/natural-play-area-lets-childrens-imaginations-run; wildrock.org

A Secret Rose Garden atlasobscura.com/places/new-dominion-bookshop-rose-garden

Discover Latin Social Dancing zabordance.com

A Congregation with History gracekeswick.org/history.html; en.wikipedia.org/wiki/William_Strickland_(architect)

Blessed Be the Cheese olamonastery.org/cheese-making/history-of-our-industry; eatingeurope.com/blog/dutch-gouda-cheese

Marked by These Monuments nytimes.com/2020/09/12/us/charlottesville-confederate-statue-at-ready.html; washingtonpost.com/lifestyle/2019/08/20/two-women-lead-free-tour-charlottesvilles-confederate-monuments-each-month-new-website-lets-everyone-listen; cvilletomorrow.org/articles/johnny-reb-is-gone-heres-the-status-of-the-5-other-charlottesville-area-statues-activists-want-removed; dailyprogress.com/news/local/crime-and-courts/state-supreme-court-focuses-on-retroactivity-of-statues-law-during-charlottesville-hearing/article_b4f89380-2068-11eb-b46b-4bc6a49221a0.html

Slave Auction block marker c-ville.com/no-harm-intended-county-resident-confesses-to-taking-slave-auction-block; en.wikipedia.org/wiki/Robert_E._Lee_Monument_(Charlottesville,_Virginia)

Rare Art Collection en.wikipedia.org/wiki/Kluge-Ruhe_Aboriginal_Art_Collection; kluge-ruhe.org/education/essential-introduction-aboriginal-art-25-facts; aboriginal-art-australia.com/aboriginal-art-library/the-story-of-aboriginal-art

Help from Hollywood c-ville.com/haven-on-earth-homeless-shelter-welcomes-public-for-lunch-and-feeds-your-soul-too

Dave Matthews Band Tour tips2liveby.com/post/charlottesville-a-guide-to-the-city-and-the-9-places-every-dmb-fan-must-visit; redlightmanagement.com/how-dave-matthews-gives-back-to-his-hometown-of-charlottesville

A Memorial to John Henry James wolfe-brendan.medium.com/the-train-at-woods-crossing-caa9d72d03c1; washingtonpost.com/local/sacred-ground-now-reclaimed-a-charlottesville-story/2018/07/07/a2d12d0c-7e12-11e8-b0ef-fffcabeff946_story.html; c-ville.com/confronting-shameful-past-search-1898-lynching-site-narrows; brendanwolfe.com/lynching

From Garden to Glass fifthseasongardening.com/blog

Catch a Concert sprintpavilion.com

Michoacán Specialties culinarybackstreets.com/cities-category/mexico-city/2018/a-treat-from-tocumbo; archivo.eluniversal.com.mx/nacion/194919.html; eater.com/2019/10/22/20908347/la-michoacana-paleta-legal-battle; laflormichoacana.com/menu

A Barn Under a Bridge barbiesburritobarn.com; dailyprogress.com/news/local/q-a-with-barbie-brannock-of-barbies-burrito-barn/article_3d663472-9b40-11e7-b23d-47e996f70c5f.html

LARP at Darden Towe Park dailyprogress.com/news/local/local-larp-group-leads-to-camaraderie-brings-family-together/article_751d3726-8d2a-11e8-806a-8789ff82bbf2.html; zornvongal.com

Acknowledging History washingtonpost.com/goingoutguide/museums/a-powerful-new-memorial-to-u-vas-enslaved-workers-reclaims-lost-lives-and-forgotten-narratives/2020/08/12/7be63e66-dc03-11ea-b205-ff838e15a9a6_story.html; slavery.virginia.edu/memorial-for-enslaved-laborers; architecturaldigest.com/story/uva-memorial-to-enslaved-laborers; www2.virginia.edu/slaverymemorial

Bike a Mountain mtbproject.com/trail/7006227/preddy-creek-loop; cambc.org/trail-information/127-2

Water Therapy ilovecville.com/12-reasons-to-float-at-aquafloat-near-the-downtown-mall; aquafloatcville.com

Clandestine Cocktails tavernandgrocery.com/lost-saint; alleylight.com

Time-Travel to a Soda Fountain facebook.com/timberlakesdrugstore; video.vpm.org/video/timberlakes-drug-store-3cvfnu

Book a Tiny Hotel readthehook.com/79790/onarchitecture-star-reborn-jefferson-readied-next-act; jeffhotel.com; thetownsmanhotel.com

Get Your Hands Dirty silkmillspm.com/history-2; cityclaycville.com

Witness a Spectacle clawville.org; washingtonpost.com/wp-dyn/content/story/2010/02/26/ST2010022606090.html?sid=ST2010022606090; southernladiesarmwrestling.com/about-teams

Private Collection Goes Public decadesarcade.com; dailyprogress.com/news/local/new-arcade-brings-classic-pinball-games-to-charlottesville/article_da9aec44-2982-11e8-97f3-eb773ba57f57.html

When Elizabeth Taylor Came to Town small.library.virginia.edu/collections/featured/the-holsinger-studio-collection; dailyprogress.com/125yearsofprogress/hollywood-in-charlottesville-elizabeth-taylor-rock-hudson-and-james-dean-were-in-town-in-1955/article_44c1698e-4574-11e7-bd17-1f9813e48959.html; albemarlehistory.org/people

Choose Your Own Path en.wikipedia.org/wiki/Biscuit_Run_State_Park; c-ville.com/Taxpayer_State_Park; readthehook.com/101906/flip-flopped-biscuit-run-men-want-20-million-more-taxpayers; cvillepedia.org/images/20110801-BiscuitRunConcept.jpg

The Steeple with No People c-ville.com/its-a-neighborhood-thing-the-ghostly-past-and-uncertain-future-of-woolen-mills-chapel

Take a Dip hikingupward.com/SNP/RiprapHollow; c-ville.com/hidden-spots-will-keep-cool-summer; virginiavinesandtrails.wordpress.com/2015/07/26/snake-hole

Railway Landmark c-ville.com/the-charlottesville-coal-tower; c-ville.com/slow-going-water-street-coal-tower-restoration-project-at-a-standstill

A River Runs Through It rivannarivercompany.com; cvillepedia.org/Rivanna_River

Obscure Eatery c-ville.com/tried-and-true-tastings-of-charlottesville; charlottesville29.com/2017/11/03/five-finds-on-friday-wilson-richey-2; dailyprogress.com/archives/dont-be-fooled---tastings-is-more-than-a-wine-shop/article_e4aecd5a-b6c2-11e7-a2dc-77a54c68437b.html

The House That Barringer Built c-ville.com/scattered-history-the-citys-74-historic-properties-piece-together-our-past; housing.virginia.edu/area/1141; pages.shanti.virginia.edu/FH_Collaboration/2016/09/16/faq

Wine Through Time themonticellowinecompany.com; publishing.cdlib.org/ucpressebooks; dailyprogress.com/business/couple-reviving-monticello-wine-company-label-to-give-the-city-its-own-brand/article_0bf97a55-44be-5f07-a441-89fbd15e6366.html; timesofindia.indiatimes.com/travel/eating-out/the-birthplace-of-american-wine-the-untold-story-behind-virginias-vines/as79581344.cms

White Deer Sightings blog.nature.org/science/2016/02/03/white-deer-understanding-a-common-animal-of-uncommon-color; nyantler-outdoors.com/piebald-deer.html; crystalwind.ca/walking-the-red-road/meaning-and-legend-of-the-white-deer

Get a Confidence Booster places.singleplatform.com/phoenix-dance-studio; insidehook.com/daily_brief/movies/netflix-pole-dancing-documentary-strippers

Have a Feast! feastvirginia.com

Secret Sledding Hills c-ville.com/way-winter-7-charlottesville-sledding-spots

Climb Aboard a Keelboat washingtonpost.com/history/2020/01/12/york-slave-lewis-clark-expedition; monacannation.com/our-history.html; lewisandclarkvirginia.org; lewisandclarkvirginia.org/visitus

Off-Season Football virginiasilverbacks.com/teams/default.asp?p=schedule&u=VIRGINIASILVERBACKS&s=football; news.virginia.edu/content/video-professor-day-placekicker-weekends

Tiny Concert Venue thegaragecville.com/#shows

The Real Highland dailyprogress.com/news/local/monroe-s-home-restores-its-original-name-highland/article_e958c4d8-088a-11e6-9323-c7e781f4c73c.html; wm.edu/sites/highland/index.php

'Hoos House, or Campbell House on Lewis Mountain lewismountainva.com; cavalierdaily.com/article/2006/11/hoos-house; willtownes.wordpress.com/2013/04/05/charlottesville-mystery-house; readthehook.com/103887/eugene-bradbury

Untoasted Favorite; charlottesville29.com/bodos; cvillepedia.org/Bodo%27s_Bagels

Tiny Window, Big Flavors vunoodles.com/product/vietnamese-iced-coffee/92?cs=true&cst=custom

A Walk in the Woods readthehook.com/108746/foxhaven-could-be-nature-haven; newsadvance.com/nelson_county_times/news/remembering-a-lover-of-the-land-and-mountains/article_92e4fdb1-1f5d-5f6e-a99c-f00550151b47.html

Urban Treasure Hunt geocaching.com/play

Georgia O'Keeffe Slept Here hmdb.org/m.asp?m=19092; news.virginia.edu/content/virginia-years-untold-story-georgia-okeeffes-time-uva; en.wikipedia.org/wiki/O%27Keeffe_at_the_University_of_Virginia,_1912%E2%80%931914

Is That Tony Hawk? cvilletomorrow.org/articles/skateboarder-tony-hawk-makes-gift-for-skate-park; wealthygorilla.com/tony-hawk-net-worth

Hoops with a Message cardinalsbasketball.com

The Hungry, Truck-Eating Bridge twitter.com/uvacornerbridge?lang=en

Real Neapolitan-Style Pizza lampopizza.com

Tea and Hookah Nook teabazaar.com

Board Games with a Local Connection npr.org/2018/09/12/643305137/a-farm-to-table-board-game-for-manure-audiences-only

Snuggle a Goat washingtonpost.com/news/local/wp/2016/01/11/this-farm-needs-volunteers-to-snuggle-with-its-baby-goats-this-winter

Get Around Town for Free charlottesville.gov/481/CAT-Schedules-Maps

Look at the Sky Above astro.virginia.edu; astronomy.as.virginia.edu/research/observatories/mccormick

Charlottesville's Olive Garden richmond.com/food-drink/why-isnt-there-an-olive-garden-in-charlottesville-it-s-complicated/article_c0412a64-6c4a-5c0e-95f6-760b0fa2c170.html

Behind the Scenes at Monticello funinfairfaxva.com/charlottesville-getaway-virginia; monticello.org

Serpentine Walls cavalierdaily.com/article/2020/04/new-virginia-athletics-logo-ignites-controversy-over-use-of-serpentine-walls#:~:text=The%20serpentine%20walls%20were%20originally,quarters%20of%20slaves%20from%20view; encyclopediavirginia.org/entries/emmet-john-patten-1796-1842; c-ville.com/great-spots-17-charlottesvilles-intriguing-places; news.virginia.edu/illimitable/ingenuity/if-these-walls-could-talk

Under the Blue Ridge nelsoncounty.com/wanderlove/crozet-tunnel-greenway; c-ville.com/tunnel-vision; asce.org/project/crozet-s-blue-ridge-tunnel

Art to Experience dailyprogress.com/news/local/love-butt-finds-permanent-home-at-ix-art-park/article_f6cd1148-5037-11e5-a0d4-cf61cf2c20a0.html; gardenandgun.com/feature/artist-residence-beatrix-osts-virginia-estate

Nature, Preserved cvillepedia.org/River_View_Farm

Cold War Military Bunkers washingtonpost.com/politics/2020/06/01/what-we-know-about-white-houses-secret-bunkers-tunnels; nypost.com/2017/06/10/this-is-where-the-government-will-hide-during-a-nuclear-war; garrettgraff.com/books/raven-rock; phasezero.gawker.com/the-secret-mountain-our-spies-will-hide-in-when-washing-1701044312; wikimapia.org/98088/AT-T-Project-Office-Peters-Mountain-Virginia; wikimapia.org/1863131/AT-T-Cold-War-Project-Office-Microwave-Communications-Bunker; coldwar-c4i.net/ATT_Project/Buckingham/index.html

Get in Some Steps monticello.org/visit/the-saunders-monticello-trail

Urban Hiking Adventures rivannatrails.org; visitcharlottesville.org/listing/rivanna-trail/1125

Gas Station Goodies crossroadcornershops.com

A History Walk with a Ghostly Spin dailyprogress.com/125yearsofprogress/former-mayor-hanged-this-day-in-1905-marking-last-execution-in-charlottesville/article_e003494a-efa1-11e6-bc2e-276cc4eae5e6.html

Horsing Around vapolo.org; kingfamilyvineyards.com/polo

Little Free Libraries littlefreelibrary.org/ourmap; mapping.littlefreepantry.org/pantry/1306

Murals All Over Town charlottesvillemuralproject.org/map

Edible Landscaping ediblelandscaping.com/about.php

Honor Fallen Firefighters en.wikipedia.org/wiki/Emergency_workers_killed_in_the_September_11_attacks; dailyprogress.com/news/local/charlottesville-9-11-memorial-finds-home-in-fire-station/article_b252894c-37e8-11e5-bc05-5b1f90549082.html

Chicken Strip cvillepedia.org/Charlottesville_League_of_Urban_Chicken_Keepers

Peek at The Farm uvamagazine.org/articles/a_civil_occupation; encyclopediavirginia.org/9826-9c9bb40037e4bf4; tjrs.monticello.org/letter/2633; en.wikipedia.org/wiki/Lewis_Farm; cvillepedia.org/The_Farm_(property)

Fry's Spring Beach Club: Private Club Making Amends frysspring.org/fsnc

The Extras at Montpelier bbvwine.com; findagrave.com/memorial/661/james-madison; en.wikipedia.org/wiki/Montpelier_(Orange,_Virginia)#The_duPont_family; fallfiberfestival.org

The Secret to Great Local Fishing albemarleangler.com/private-water

INDEX